P +i
YAM.

INDUSTRIAL DESIGN FOR ENGINEERS

WITHDRAWN

INDUSTRIAL DESIGN FOR ENGINEERS

W. H. MAYALL, C.Eng., A.F.R.Ae.S

LONDON   ILIFFE BOOKS LTD.

© W. H. Mayall, 1967
First published in 1967 by Iliffe Books Ltd.,
Dorset House, Stamford Street, London, S.E.1

Printed and bound in England by
C. Tinling & Co. Ltd., Liverpool, London and Prescot

CONTENTS

PREFACE

THIS book has been prepared to meet a growing interest in the subject of industrial design in relation to the design of engineering equipment. There are several reasons for this. One is that closer studies of the whole design process prove that industrial design must be taken into account if design work is to be undertaken in a comprehensive manner. Another and connected reason is that a better-looking, easier-to-use product is a more attractive sales proposition. A third and again connected reason is that engineers are realising more and more the need to produce goods which, while performing specified tasks, will be satisfactory both in use and in their influence upon human environments.

It may be argued that those who produce industrial equipment have a compelling reason for recognising this need; that people at work should be shown the greatest consideration. But too often in the past, machines appear to have been designed with little respect for those who have to use them. Perhaps this book can play a small part in encouraging further improvements. Ideally these improvements should be married either to machines whose technical performance is being improved or to newly emerging machines embodying new principles. It is not the purpose of industrial design to disguise a lack of technical advancement. Therefore this book is mainly addressed to those who are, or will be, concerned with making technical advances. If they are aware of the aspects it describes then they will be able to deal with these aspects with greater efficiency.

But, and most important, this is not a book on how to become proficient in industrial design work. No book can do this, for proficiency depends upon practice. Its main purpose is to explain the factors involved and to describe their relationship both to each other and to other factors in the engineering design process. In order to do this a structure has been devised based on seeing design as fulfilling a spectrum of requirements within a framework of available resources. But this structure is used only for explanatory purposes. It would be quite possible to devise another type of structure.

My reason for using it here is that it has found acceptance by those engineers with whom I have had the privilege of discussing industrial design during courses and lectures on the subject. My thanks must go first to them for encouraging me to prepare this book, then to my colleagues in our common effort and finally to those industrial designers who are engaged in the worthwhile task of helping to make engineering products fit for people.

W.H.M.

South Nutfield, Surrey, 1966.

Chapter One

AN APPROACH TO
INDUSTRIAL DESIGN

MAN became a designer as soon as he began to modify the form of natural objects. A stick hardened by fire to make a spear, or a stone roughly chipped for cutting, beating or digging were probably his first products. Chosen to suit his own form and actions, stick or stone were altered to make them more effective for the task in mind. No doubt the first rudimentary hand-axes were made from stones chosen both because they could be manipulated and because they had some semblance of a cutting edge. Early man would then improve this cutting edge so far as his skill, the tools at his disposal—in this case other stones—and the material qualities of the emerging axe would permit.

As he became more proficient, early man produced hand-axes by segmenting larger stones. Here, quite intuitively, he resolved two requirements in making his product. He cut to produce a sharp edged form and he cut to produce something he could manipulate. But it may be that even before he produced these so-called cored axes, he chipped his stones to achieve another aim. Professor Gordon Childe has remarked that, as long ago as Neanderthal man, flints appear to have been fashioned 'with more care and delicacy than was requisite for mere utilitarian efficiency . . . it looks as if their author had wanted to make an implement that was not only serviceable but also beautiful'. If this is so, early man intuitively built a third requirement into his product.

9

With the hand-axe in mind, these three requirements could be defined as follows:

A TECHNICAL REQUIREMENT concerned with the cutting capacity of the axe,

An ERGONOMIC REQUIREMENT concerned with the user's ability to hold and manipulate the axe,

An AESTHETIC REQUIREMENT concerned with the effect of the axe's form upon the user's inner feelings.

All man's products could be examined in relation to these three requirements. Clearly every product must embody a technical requirement. The technical requirement in designing a chair is that it should be structurally safe and stable; in a machine tool that it should provide specified cutting facilities possibly for a foreseen period of time. Most products embody an ergonomic requirement. A chair must not only support the sitter safely, it must support him comfortably. A machine tool must not only perform specified cutting operations, it must be capable of being operated. Some products, for example electric motors or transformers, do not require human manipulation to perform their duties. Nevertheless they have to be handled when installed and maintained, so that the ergonomic requirement is still present. Coming to the aesthetic requirement, some products show that their designers have aimed to give aesthetic satisfaction, others suggest that this requirement has been ignored. But all give rise to some form of aesthetic response, whether favourable or unfavourable, whether consciously aimed for or not. This is an important point. For example some aircraft or boats inspire strong aesthetic appreciation yet their forms may have emerged almost entirely from seeking solutions to technical requirements. Other products gain aesthetic appreciation when their forms have been largely determined by ergonomic requirements. Here the traditional mowing scythe is a case in point.

However, common experience shows that aesthetic satisfaction does not always arise when technical and ergonomic aims have been realised. This is largely because there are many products whose forms cannot or need not be precisely determined by these requirements. Variations are possible and in such cases one would expect product designers to aim to meet the aesthetic requirement when undertaking design work.

1.1 ELEMENTS OF DESIGN

In designing any product, requirements are inevitably interlinked in one way or another. Taking the stone axe as an example, the three main requirements, technical, ergonomic and aesthetic are each determined by the following characteristics:

1. TECHNICAL REQUIREMENT (i.e. cutting capacity of the axe): sharpness, length of cutting edge, weight, size, shape, material strength and applied force.
2. ERGONOMIC REQUIREMENT (i.e. handling qualities): weight, size, shape, texture and reacted force.
3. AESTHETIC REQUIREMENT (i.e. visual and possibly tactile appeal of the axe): size, shape, texture and colour.

It can be seen that certain characteristics such as shape and size influence all requirements. When this occurs it may be necessary to make adjustments so that a particular characteristic meets two or more requirements. For example with the stone axe, an increase in size would, in theory, improve its cutting capacity. But this increase in size might make the tool difficult to hold and manipulate. Thus the designer seeks a size considered to be most effective for fulfilling both requirements. This process of adjustment has frequently been termed a process of compromise and is an important part of a designer's skill for it usually involves considering more than two requirements when determining any characteristic.

While some characteristics fulfil two or more requirements others may appear to be relatively independent. Thus the axe could have varying degrees of sharpness in achieving the technical requirement without having a profound influence on ergonomic or aesthetic needs. Or it could have different colours to meet aesthetic needs without influencing technical or ergonomic requirements. But it could not have any degree of sharpness nor any colour its designer might conceive. Sharpness cannot be greater than the material qualities of the axe, its creator's skill and the tools at his disposal will allow. Colours cannot be used other than those which are available and which can be made to adhere to and remain upon the axe. The designer is always limited by the materials, tools and skills at his disposal. These provide the framework within which he creates his product. And the history of product development is very largely the history of enlarging this framework; from the use of stones and the crude chippings of early man to the diversity of natural and synthetic materials, the powered tools and the specialised skills of today. Therefore a second aspect of the designer's skill is that he should know the limitations within which he must create his product.

Frequently, particularly today when more materials, more tools and more skills are available, limitations are self-imposed rather than externally imposed. For example, early man might have been able to produce a very sharp axe but found that for all practical purposes it was unnecessary to go beyond a certain sharpness. A modern designer might call for a certain degree of surface finish, believing it to be adequate for the purpose in mind, though knowing that a higher degree of finish could be obtained. Today, limitations are generally imposed by the need to achieve a specified cost or perhaps to meet a required manufacturing time. Few products are designed regardless of cost and the time needed to produce them.

Limitations, either imposed on the designer or self-imposed, lead to another important aspect of the art of designing. This is that the designer may give an order of importance to the various requirements he is seeking to meet. It is to be expected that an effective solution to technical requirements would take precedence, to be followed by attainment of ergonomic requirements and then acknowledgement of aesthetic needs. But this does not imply that a designer will first solve the technical problem and then proceed to adapt his solution to ergonomic needs. As may be observed from the analysis of the stone axe, the inter-relationship of characteristics demands that all requirements be borne in mind literally at the same time; even though they may be given different values. This is the essential part of the art of designing. Thus when assessing how well a product meets any one requirement, other requirements cannot be ignored. At base, the merit of a product rests on how well its characteristics combine to meet all requirements within the limitations imposed upon its designer.

In order to picture this basic nature of design, namely the blending or synthesis of requirements into one unit, design might be likened to a colour spectrum. The simple analysis of the stone axe identified three requirements, but it is clear that these merge with one another as do the colours of the spectrum. The three main requirements might be regarded as primary colours which could be broken down into further colours. In other words the spectrum can be expanded. Thus within the technical requirement, account could be taken of expected life, performance in specified ambient conditions, accuracy of operation etc.—factors which are highly relevant today but which were probably of less interest to early man. Similarly, breakdowns in ergonomic and aesthetic requirements might be made. This spectrum analogy may also be useful in picturing the relative importance of the various requirements which have to be blended into a product, and which the designer must determine before he begins his work.

With this concept in mind, the importance and character of the aesthetic requirement in the history of product design can now be briefly surveyed.

1.2 AESTHETICS IN THE HISTORY OF PRODUCT DESIGN

Obviously early man had no thought for the foregoing abstractions. He blended his requirements within his limitations in a completely intuitive manner. Indeed many designers still do so today. As man increased his skill, found new materials and created new tools so his products became both more diverse in character and more specialised in themselves. His products evolved. He made technical advances, as when putting a handle to his stone axe to increase its striking power. He made ergonomic advances; a shaped handle to improve grip. And he paid more attention to aesthetic needs. It would be reasonable to suppose that products usually evolved in this way: technical requirements were met first and then products became more refined in ergonomic and aesthetic terms. While it would not be difficult to find examples of this kind of evolution, products can be found which appear to indicate a combined development. The earliest known pottery appears to have been decorated by marks probably produced by a stick before the clay was dried out in the sun. It might be argued that aesthetic needs were realised when product materials could be easily manipulated. Thus clay and wood would be more amenable than the early metals copper, bronze and later iron. But another aspect presents itself; in effect that of the degree of importance which man gave to aesthetic needs in the products he used. It is clear that he paid more attention to the products with which he lived than to those with which he worked. Products which would now be called durable consumer products, furniture, textiles and pottery, received much more aesthetic interest than products used for manufacturing, hunting and later farming.

As man moved from hunter to agrarian, so he became more settled and devised products which gave him comfort as well as protection. The beginnings of specialisation occurred as the farmer, producing more than he needed to sustain himself, exchanged his surplus food for implements and utensils made by those with greater expertise. Early settlements created initially for mutual protection became centres of trade. They also became centres of power whether administered in a temporal or a spiritual sense by the rulers of early societies. The rulers gathered possessions which, both in number and in kind, helped to distinguish them from their subjects. And these possessions came to embody qualities which not only gave aesthetic pleasure but also added to their owners' distinction. To paraphrase Professor Childe, it might be said that the creators of such products went beyond what might have been needed for pure aesthetic appreciation, they endeavoured to produce goods which could signify status. Indeed where the social leaders either devised or were assigned symbols by which to identify themselves, such symbols might well be incorporated into the design of their possessions.

On the whole, products used in man's working life stood outside this type of development. They also remained fairly static in form, though becoming more refined as new materials and skills were developed. Meantime other products changed markedly in character though not in basic purpose. For example in the history of furniture, pronounced changes in style occurred partly as new materials and methods of construction appeared, partly in relation to environmental influences, notably architecture, and partly as society's needs changed. But the basic forms of many tools remained almost unaltered over many centuries. Elementary forerunners of some modern machines such as the lathe or the loom were conceived, but progress was limited by the lack of any really powerful yet controllable source of energy. Power came only from man himself, from trained beasts or from those capricious elements wind and water.

This situation was to undergo a dramatic change when steam power began to be used towards the end of the eighteenth century. While the

Industrial Revolution did not begin with the arrival of the steam engine, it can be fairly said that steam started a new phase, not only in the history of product design but also in the history of society. Steam began to drive the more complex machines emerging first in the manufacture of textiles. It began to drive tools devised to manufacture the engines which used it. And it produced a wholly new transport system; the railway. Quite suddenly a new type of product appeared. This product, the powered machine, demanded much more skill from its designer in seeking to achieve technical requirements. As it developed, so the demand for what would now be called technical expertise became increasingly more intense. By the middle of the nineteenth century, the application of the physical sciences began to replace earlier empiricism and this led both to new products and to new sources of power, notably electrical power. The degree of expertise needed to solve the technical requirements in the design of these products almost compelled their designers to concentrate on these requirements, not to the exclusion of others, but certainly without such a deep concern for them. Machinery was clumsy and frequently dangerous to operate. Little attention was paid to aesthetics, except for occasional attempts to apply forms or idioms which happened to be in vogue in the architecture or domestic products of the time. And when they were applied, such borrowed forms sat rather sadly on the powerful forms of the emerging machines. On the whole the machine remained what might now be called strictly functional; becoming more refined as more refined solutions were found to technical requirements rather than by paying very much more attention to ergonomic and aesthetic needs. The reasons for this are fairly clear. Tools had never been so highly regarded as domestic products and there was no reason why there should be any change when powered tools began to appear. Further, these tools were in an embryonic state. They might be compared with the first stages in the development of early man's stone axe.

But the new machines and the factory system which grew up around them had a profound effect upon furniture, furnishings and other domestic products. Producing in greater quantities, these machines could also reproduce ornamentation which though skilfully used to enhance the products of the late eighteenth and earlier nineteenth centuries, began to overpower the products of the middle to late nineteenth century. Such over-embellishment was eagerly sought by an enlarging middle class anxious to achieve social distinction by way of its possessions. In this situation nobody noticed the paradox of one class of designer, the emerging mechanical engineer, concentrating almost entirely on the technical end of the design spectrum, while another class of designer concentrated on design aspects which might appear to be beyond this spectrum altogether, in that they were concerned with status and style as much as with giving aesthetic pleasure. Just as this paradox went unnoticed, so did the aesthetic disparity between machine and domestic product for, on the whole, they occupied different worlds.

Such was the situation in the mid-nineteenth century. It was to take another century before the aesthetic standard of man's working environment came to be regarded as important. Over this period, great social changes were accompanied by changes in the character of domestic products.

These changes emerged from several sources; from a revulsion for the over-ornate products of the late nineteenth century, from changes in the way people lived, particularly as machinery began to appear in the domestic world, and from changes in the way products were made, notably through the introduction of mass-production techniques.

Towards the end of the nineteenth century, an American architect, Louis Sullivan, coined the phrase 'form follows function'. It was an apt directive for ensuing trends. Initially the new styles introduced by pioneering twentieth-century architects and domestic product designers seemed almost clinical by comparison with those of earlier periods. Devoid of decoration their aesthetic appeal depended upon their form; and this form was determined in a manner which would best display the products function. It is important that this should be recognised. It is sometimes supposed that this so-called functional style was obtained solely by meeting technical, or technical and ergonomic requirements. This was not in fact the case simply because a variety of 'functional' solutions could easily be produced for the types of product taking on the new and, to some people, somewhat austere form. In effect 'form follows function' was a directive leading to solutions which would display the product's purpose in the simplest terms.

1.3 INDUSTRIAL DESIGN

It was during the emergence of this so-called functional style that the expression 'industrial design' began to be used to describe the design of products making up the domestic scene. This expression made sense when related to products which had been previously made by craft processes and which, with the emergence of the machine, had come to be made by industrial processes. But it was, and still can be, highly confusing when applied to the design of machinery. As it is used today, not only does 'industrial design' appear confusing but also the word *design* appears to have a different meaning from that with which the engineer is familiar. This difficulty is resolved in some degree by recognising the unfortunate schism which tended to develop in design in the nineteenth century. The engineer tended to regard design in terms of achieving solutions to technical requirements, while the domestic product designer, later to become the industrial designer, saw design in terms of achieving aesthetic requirements. In this respect he tended to link the word design with its use in art where it can be interpreted in a number of ways from describing a pattern to signifying the composition or structure of a painting.

In a sense, the difference of interpretation was bound to occur. The engineer was necessarily confined to technical aspects in view of the greater expertise needed to deal with them. On the other hand the forerunner of the industrial designer was dealing with products which, comparatively speaking, were technically simple with a long evolutionary history over which aesthetic satisfaction had been constantly sought. Thus as an initial approach, industrial design could be described as design biased towards the aesthetic end of the design spectrum and concerned with products made by industrial processes. On the other hand engineering design is still strongly biased, however reluctant some engineers may be to admit it, towards the technical end of the design spectrum. Indeed, though both types of designer may object, it is only recently that the full range of design has come to be appreciated.

This has partly come about as industrial designers began to work first on machinery coming into the domestic world and then, with improvements in working conditions, on machinery used in factories and other places of work. In order to work effectively both with engineers and within the limitations imposed by materials and manu-

B

facturing processes, training systems for industrial designers working on engineering products began to develop. These are now known as industrial design (engineering) courses to distinguish them from industrial design courses dealing with products once made by craft processes; that is furniture, metalware or pottery.

The emergence of industrial design (engineering) courses and the introduction of the industrial designer into engineering has been viewed sceptically by some engineers. This may be because they are deeply entrenched in the belief that design is concerned only with achieving a technical solution which, when found, will fully satisfy aesthetic requirements, or possibly because they feel quite competent to deal with aesthetic aspects and see no need for assistance. Since some products do create considerable aesthetic pleasure and yet are formed almost entirely according to technical requirements (as stated earlier, some aircraft and boats), and since many engineers have produced goods which display aesthetic sensibility, it is not surprising that those who resist the industrial designer should voice these facts and assert that he is unnecessary. Regrettably they overlook the many products which lack aesthetic quality and which are to be found mainly in the field of manufacturing and associated equipment, namely the field of capital goods.

The engineer may readily call upon the services of a stress analyst; regarding him as bringing specialist knowledge to the design task. He should regard the industrial designer in precisely the same way; not as a usurper nor as 'the designer'—unfortunately an impression sometimes created by the industrial designer himself or by those who wish to encourage him. Design today, in the sense that it is the process which determines the whole nature of a product and not one or more partial aspects, is becoming more and more the work of a team. But the team can only work effectively if each member is aware of the abilities and aims of his colleagues.

1.4 A STRUCTURE FOR INDUSTRIAL DESIGN IN ENGINEERING

The movement of industrial designers into the field of capital goods has had a significant influence. It has tended to produce a more profound view of the industrial designer's purpose. Manufacturing machines, however complex, are still basically tools. Their purpose is to produce goods at minimum cost and with minimum expenditure of effort. While these aims guide the engineer in the way in which he seeks technical solutions to the design problem, they also guide the industrial designer. That is, when determining forms and colours, the industrial designer will aim to assist those who have to operate or maintain the equipment. Thus the aim is not only to generate aesthetic satisfaction but also to help produce ergonomic convenience. The common factor in these two aims is of course, the human being. As the American industrial designer, Henry Dreyfuss, has put it, the industrial designer is 'designing for people'.

In order to manipulate form and colour in an ergonomic sense, data derived from scientific studies of human behaviour in the control of machines has been used by industrial designers. This data has also come to be increasingly used by industrial designers concerned with the so-called craft-basis products—especially furniture. Here in particular, data on human dimensions have assisted the design of chairs, tables, desks and the like. Thus in the design of both consumer and capital goods the industrial designer's aim has come to be interpreted as providing human beings not merely with aesthetic satisfaction but with products which suit and appeal to them at every point of contact.

Visualising a design spectrum running from technical requirements, through ergonomic requirements to aesthetic needs, it might be said that industrial design in engineering is embracing more of this spectrum than hitherto. At the same time engineering design is also embracing more of the spectrum, since the importance of ergonomic aspects is being increasingly recognised by engineers. The development might be considered on a somewhat more philosophical level in order to outline a structure for industrial design in relation to engineering products.

When Thomas Treadgold wrote his famous definition of an engineer, he used the expression 'for the use and convenience of Man' to describe the engineer's purpose in 'directing the great sources of power in nature'. Treadgold believed that the emerging machines would enhance man's life and undoubtedly the phrase 'use and convenience . . .' was a somewhat rhetorical allusion to this belief. However, perhaps more by accident than intention, Treadgold hit upon two concepts which, are relevant to any type of product. First and foremost, a product is constructed for human use. It performs, or helps man to perform a task. The task may be a simple one, such as supporting him in a semi-reclining position, or it may be complex such as producing answers to equations which might otherwise require a lifetime to solve. A chair which collapses or a computer which fails to operate has no value. But while the fundamental purpose of products is to be of use, they should also be convenient for those who use them. And this convenience should stretch from meeting ergonomic needs to providing a satisfactory environment in which to live and work.

Taking Treadgold's phrase, the engineer is clearly responsible for combining 'use and convenience' in his products. But, as pointed out earlier, he has been virtually forced to concentrate on meeting technical requirements. In other words he has of necessity been aiming primarily, and indeed properly, to produce devices for human use. A very general distinction between the engineer and the industrial designer might therefore be made as follows:

1. The *engineering designer* is biased towards producing goods which have 'use', in the sense that they perform specified tasks.
2. The *industrial designer* is biased towards ensuring that 'useful' products satisfy and appeal to their users.

Clearly these aims must be accepted in a very broad light. They should not be regarded as defining specific functions. Nor should they suggest that the engineer provides the 'technical' answers while the industrial designer provides the 'human' answers. In by far the majority of cases, and unless the product is comparatively simple, the industrial designer is simply a member of the engineering team. Moreover there are obvious overlaps in the two aims. The subject of ergonomics is as important to the engineering designer as it is to the industrial designer. The analysis of characteristics in early man's stone axe showed that the attainment of the three primary aims in product design cannot be treated separately. Solution of the technical requirement cannot be achieved without knowledge of ergonomic needs. Today this is particularly the case in the design of mechanical equipment controlled by handwheels, levers and the like. Again it is so even when designing electrical or electronic circuitry, for though the basis of the design may be a circuit diagram, components have to be located so that they can be controlled and serviced. Finally each designer is bounded by the limitations within which design work must be undertaken, and which today would be called either available or nominated materials, plant and labour resources. In practice therefore each designer's aims are bound to intertwine. Indeed the best work has been achieved when this has been encouraged.

Nevertheless the foregoing broad distinction helps to produce a structure for industrial design so that the subject can be examined in relation to the design of engineering products. Taking Henry Dreyfuss's statement 'designing for people' as the basic aim:

1. Products must satisfy people in the ergonomic sense.
2. Products should satisfy the natural human need for beauty; a word somewhat out of fashion, but still the essential basis of the aesthetic requirement.
3. Products may have to satisfy other human needs, perhaps even more tenuous than the desire for beauty, but nevertheless real, as the history of product development shows. Thus a product with a particular style may be sought because it appeals to the user in forming his environment; because it may, in his eyes, signify his status; or because it may be regarded as signifying the reputable nature of its maker.

These latter aspects may be denied or even derided, but there is no doubt that they exist as much today as they did in the past. While more significant in the design of consumer products, perhaps excessively so in the design of automobiles, they have their influence upon the design of capital plant and equipment. For example, an up-to-date appearance may be sought very largely because it tends to signify up-to-date design in the technical sense. But clearly a modern appearance should not be a disguise for outmoded technical solutions. A particular style may appeal because it supports an impression which the user wishes to create. Thus a food manufacturer may choose equipment which looks hygienic. Again, however, this choice will not, or should not be made unless the equipment meets his performance requirements and financial circumstances. Finally, and becoming more significant, a capital goods purchaser may be influenced by what is now commonly termed 'house style'; that is, the attainment of common characteristics

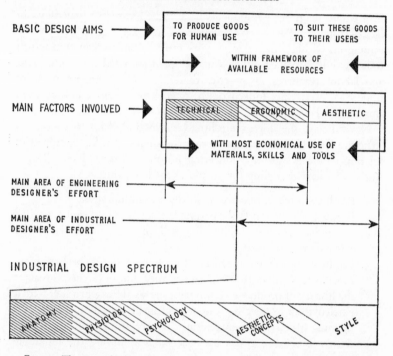

FIG. 1.1 *The scope of industrial design in designing the majority of engineering products*

both in a maker's products and in such items as catalogues, display
equipment and advertisements. These will not, in themselves, produce
a sale, but they may create a favourable impression of the maker and
this makes a sale more likely; always provided that the products are
attractive in terms of performance and price.

The spectrum concept was used as an analogy to indicate that the
various aspects of design merge into one another and can seldom be
treated as separate entities. The same analogy can be used in relation
to the aspects which constitute industrial design in engineering. In
other words there is no sharp distinction between ergonomics and
aesthetics or between aesthetics and style in whatever form the latter
is interpreted.

One definition of ergonomics is that it is concerned with the
anatomical, physiological and psychological performance of man in
a working environment. The subject of aesthetics, in that it is con-

cerned with the need for beauty, is clearly psychological in character. Thus it would be surprising if satisfaction of ergonomic needs did not merge with satisfaction of aesthetic needs. Similarly aesthetic concepts cannot be separated from considerations of style whether it reflects a particular period of time or the inclinations and standing of either user or maker. For example, it may be agreed that a product has beauty but that it does not suit the environment in which it is placed; a product of an earlier period might look out of place in a modern setting.

In short the division of industrial design into three main categories, is made purely for the sake of analysis. In practice these aspects overlap and merge together just as the general aims of the engineer and the industrial designer overlap and intertwine. The structure of industrial design in relation to the design of engineering products may be outlined as in Fig. 1.1 but it is essential that it should not be accepted as a rigid structure. Design has been called a process of synthesis, in that a number of requirements have to be met in one product. In any type of design work, adjustments or compromises have to be made in order to meet these requirements. Therefore, if only for this reason, it is impossible in the actual practice of design to treat different requirements in isolation. The foregoing structure of industrial design serves mainly to outline the main aspects of 'designing for people'. It also indicates the main link with the more technical aspects of design; namely by way of ergonomics. By moving from the more positive aspects covered by ergonomics to the more tenuous aspects of style it suggests an order of importance, which may help when making those adjustments or compromises which invariably arise. But it cannot be applied to design work as an engineer might use a formula to solve a particular problem. Its sole purpose is to assist explanation.

Chapter Two

ERGONOMICS AND INDUSTRIAL DESIGN

THE word 'ergonomics' stems from two Greek words; *ergos* meaning 'work' and *nomos* meaning 'the laws'. It was coined in 1949 by a group of British scientists concerned during the Second World War with the efficient manipulation of military equipment; particularly equipment which was comparatively new and complex such as radar. In the U.S.A. 'human engineering' is more frequently used and is perhaps a more descriptive term. On the Continent, the expression 'biotechnics' is often employed. The broadest and certainly the most common definition of ergonomics is that it is the scientific study of man in a working environment. A more specific interpretation may also be found, namely that it is concerned with the 'man/machine relationship'. However, to some extent this is a restricting interpretation since humans at work are not always dealing with machines.

The study of humans at work calls for experience in anatomy, physiology and psychology. In addition, where machines are involved the investigator must have a knowledge of the engineering sciences. Thus ergonomics might be described as a hybrid science. Due to the range of expertise which may be called upon, it is not surprising that different types of specialist should practice within its boundaries.

However, though 'ergonomics', 'human engineering' and 'biotechnics' may be comparatively new words, the whole subject stretches back through history. George Bauer, better known as Agricola, studied the ailments and difficulties of silver miners in the early part of the sixteenth century. Paracelsus also recorded information on ailments contracted in metal ore mining. At the turn of the seventeenth century Ramazzini studied working conditions and occupational diseases in a variety of trades. He has been called the father of occupational medicine.

Ergonomics might well have developed during the Industrial Revolution, for though the new power-machines brought wealth, they also produced appalling working conditions. A series of Factory Acts slowly improved these conditions and men like Charles Thackrah laid the foundations of modern industrial medicine. The following quotation from Thackrah's writings could well be regarded as a nineteenth-century form of ergonomic thinking: 'we see no plump and rosy tailors. . . . The spine is generally curved. Pulmonary consumption is also frequent. Let a hole be made in a board, of the circumference of the tailor's body, and let his seat be placed below it. The eyes and the hands will then be sufficiently near his work: his spine will not be unnaturally bent and his chest and abdomen will be free.'

But examples of this type of concern for those at work were comparatively rare though the need for study and improvement might be evident on all sides. Improvements there were indeed, but these came by way of regulations affecting safety, working periods and conditions, and through progressive technical development, rather than by formal study. Such formal study had to wait upon improvements in our knowledge of anatomy, physiology and psychology and upon the emergence of the complex control equipment which, appearing in the Second World War, has now influenced large areas of the engineering world.

Whether ergonomics is interpreted in its widest sense or in terms of the man/machine relationship, it can be roughly broken into two parts. One part may be regarded in terms of fitting man to the machine; the other with fitting the machine to man. To take a common example, it is usual for engineering trainees to learn how to operate and read a micrometer. How they are trained to do this forms one aspect of ergonomics. But the other aspect is how the micrometer is designed to enable easy operation and correct interpretation of the measurement being taken. For many years trainees have been compelled to learn to use micrometers with thimbles divided into 25 parts and barrels divided into 4 parts per unit; each unit being equal to

0·1 in. This form of division has caused unnecessary headaches for countless trainees and it is not uncommon for even the skilled user to make mistakes. Clearly a denary scale would be preferable and at least some modern micrometers now have this type of scale. Even better is the micrometer which gives a reading in numerals, but examples of this type are still comparatively rare. As a general principle it may be said that there is little point in fitting man to the machine, until one is sure that the machine is fitted to man. This then should be the joint aim of the engineering designer and the industrial designer.

It would be tempting to try to define those factors in fitting machine to man which fall into the engineer's province as against those factors which are the industrial designer's concern. However, this regimentation of responsibilities is hardly likely to encourage co-operation. And since as was seen in Chapter One, design aspects are always interlinked it is more important that both types of designer should have a common understanding of what is involved. They will then sort out their responsibilities in relation to the character of their product and their several abilities.

2.1 GENERAL APPROACH TO THE MAN/MACHINE RELATIONSHIP

Modern engineering control systems are largely based on the cybernetic principle. That is, control is effected by measuring the difference between an actual effect and the desired effect then using the measured 'error' to achieve the desired effect; the error then being nullified. In engineering, Watt's simple flyball governor was an early example of this type of control. In the human body, the control of body temperature is but one of many examples of a similar control principle.

This principle can be applied to most, though not all man/machine relationships and can be used to provide a basis for analysis. For example, suppose that a machine operator is adjusting the speed of his machine and that the speed is shown by means of a dial gauge. From the gauge reading he will decide whether the speed is too high or too low and make an appropriate movement, say on a handwheel, until the 'error' has been eliminated. The whole process can be put into diagrammatic form as in Fig. 2.1.

From this diagram it can be seen that information is sent to the

operator from a *display* (in the example a dial gauge), defined as any
source of information helping the operator to control the machine.
The operator interprets the information in relation to the performance
he requires and passes instructions back to the machine by way of its
control system, (in the example, by moving a handwheel). The control

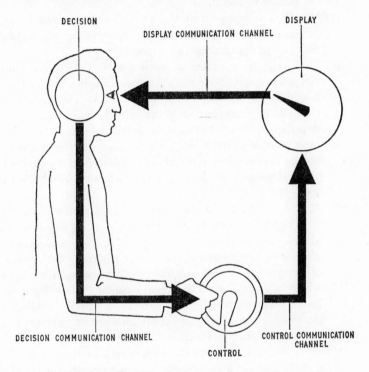

FIG. 2.1 *Elementary 'control loop' relationship between operator and machine*

movement will affect the display and the whole circulatory process will
continue until the operator finds his display matching his requirements.
Six elements determine the efficiency of this control loop.

1. There is the display which:
    (a) Must provide *all* the information needed to control the
        machine.
    (b) Must be accurate in relation to the machine's performance

(i.e. the mechanical accuracy of the dial gauge must be sufficient to allow the desired speed to be obtained).

(c) Must be clearly discerned (it is not sufficient merely to see the scale and pointer in the dial gauge, it is also necessary to distinguish clearly the scale markings and the relationship of the pointer to them).

(d) Must be intelligible (if the dial gauge used a numeral system different from that known to the operator he would find difficulty in interpreting the reading).

(e) Must help the operator to reach a correct decision (if the dial gauge required the reading to be multiplied say by 10 or 100, then the operator is required to make a computation. He could either neglect to do this or make an error).

2. There is the display communication channel which:

(a) Must provide a direct path from the display to the operator's sensory organs when he is making a related control movement (the dial gauge must be clearly seen when the handwheel is being operated).

(b) Must be adequate for the passage of information (since the dial gauge relies upon sight it must be adequately illuminated).

(c) Must be free from any restricting or distorting influences (in the case of the dial gauge, the display is strictly the position of the pointer against the scale. Any features on the scale which are not needed to make a reading, glare from the gauge glass or any physical obstruction partially obscuring the reading can restrict or distort the flow of information).

3. There is the operator's function of interpretation and decision which must be made with the minimum of interference (this implies that, as far as is possible, the operator should be in a 'normal' condition. His abilities may be influenced by physical conditions such as lighting, heating, ventilation and by the general character of his environment. In some circumstances, notably high altitude and space flight, pressure and gravitational force will also affect him. In addition he can be affected by relationships with his colleagues, his employers, his personal acquaintances and even by his social circumstances).

4. There is the decision communication channel which, in a similar manner to the display communication channel must:

(a) Have a direct path to the control element when sensing the relevant display.

(b) Be adequate to effect control.

(c) Be free from restricting or distorting influences.

5. There is the control element which must:

(a) Be capable of operation (in the case of the handwheel, it must not only be located conveniently in relation to the operator, it must be of a form which is suited to the decision communication channel; in this case, arm and hand).

(b) Move to control the machine in an expected manner particularly in relation to the display. (Thus if the handwheel must be moved say anti-clockwise to increase speed when the operator has learned from other devices that a clockwise rotation increases speed, mistakes may be encouraged. In addition, if the control has to be moved in a direction which does not relate with a movement in the display he may be further confused.) The relationship between control movement and display movement is usually called 'control compatability', see Fig. 2.2 p. 30.

6. There is the control communication channel which must be:

(a) Mechanically efficient, using 'mechanically' in its widest sense.

(b) Of a kind which will enable control compatibility.

In general it can be said that meeting the foregoing requirements will enable a control action to be undertaken correctly in minimum time and with minimum effort. Clearly the relevance of these various requirements will depend upon the type of control action envisaged. But whether the operator is filing a piece of metal or driving a car, it is possible to trace out a simple control loop. Should this be undertaken, it is important to recognise that information may reach the operator by more than one channel. For example, in filing metal, the operator receives information from seeing the file in relation to the work and also from reactions through hands and arms. Equally, a car driver may be engaged in a combined control movement as in braking, when clutch and brake pedals are operated in relation to each other.

Indeed in the majority of cases there will be more than one control loop in action during any one control movement. But while bearing this in mind it is usually possible to identify the loop which will have the most significant effect upon the operation being undertaken.

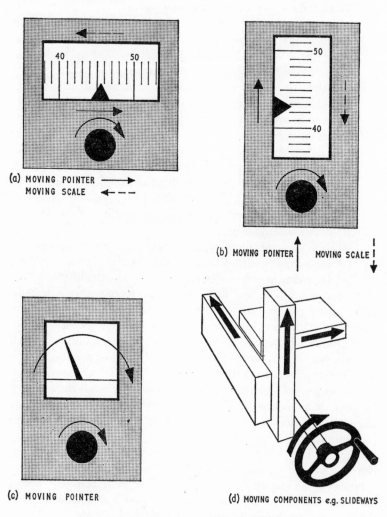

(a) MOVING POINTER ——→
MOVING SCALE ←— — —

(b) MOVING POINTER | MOVING SCALE ¦

(c) MOVING POINTER

(d) MOVING COMPONENTS *e.g.* SLIDEWAYS

FIG. 2.2 *Appropriate control-display compatibilities; more can be found in the references quoted in the Bibliography*

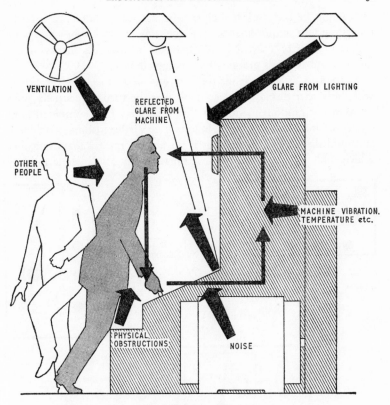

VENTILATION

REFLECTED
GLARE FROM
MACHINE

GLARE FROM LIGHTING

OTHER
PEOPLE

MACHINE VIBRATION.
TEMPERATURE etc.

PHYSICAL
OBSTRUCTIONS

NOISE

FIG. 2.3 *Factors external to the basic control loop which can affect
its efficiency*

Finally and most important, it must be recognised that each loop can
be seriously affected by external influences. The most common
external influences upon control loop efficiency are shown in Fig. 2.3.
These should always be taken into account in analysing any man/
machine activity.

2.2 MULTIPLE DISPLAY AND CONTROL
SITUATIONS

In operating a drilling machine, driving a car or setting up a computer
a variety of operations have to be performed. It is conceivable that

each might be accomplished efficiently, having paid due attention to the foregoing requirements, yet the whole operation might be inefficient. There must be an organised relationship between the displays and controls involved in a complete task.

A study of any task from the *very beginning to absolute completion*, will show that displays and controls may be used sequentially, in a more or less random manner or that there may be a combination of sequential and random control. In setting up a lathe, loading, machining and unloading a piece of bar, it is possible to trace a main sequence which, unless the lathe is fully automatic, may also include random

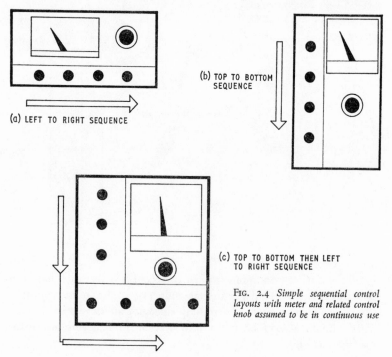

(b) TOP TO BOTTOM
SEQUENCE

(a) LEFT TO RIGHT SEQUENCE

(c) TOP TO BOTTOM THEN LEFT
TO RIGHT SEQUENCE

FIG. 2.4 *Simple sequential control layouts with meter and related control knob assumed to be in continuous use*

actions. In driving a car there are certain sequential actions but a large measure of random usage depending upon traffic conditions. But, setting up a computer may involve a definite operating sequence.

Whether a complete task involves sequential or random operation, there will usually be certain controls and displays which are more important than others. For example, some may be vital for the efficient performance of the machine, its safety and the safety of the operator. Others may only be used for periodic checking purposes. Clearly controls and displays demanding continuous use, such as the steering wheel in a car, a radar scanning screen or a lathe cross-slide handwheel, have considerable importance and must be located in the most convenient position.

Where controls and displays are used in a sequential manner, they should be laid out in a sequential pattern. This elementary requirement is often overlooked in favour of some geometrically pleasing array quite unconnected with the operating sequence. Certainly, attempts should be made to form a visually balanced control layout for a disorderly arrangement might not encourage the operator's confidence in the machine he is controlling. But while this aspect is important, particularly in relation to complex equipment, the arrangement should be firmly based upon the operating sequence.

Since for many people it is natural to scan a subject from left to right, because they learn to read in this manner, a left to right system of layout may be adopted. Alternatively a top to bottom system may be employed. Occasionally both may be used, generally when two sequential systems are involved, say one for setting up and one for actual control. However their arrangement should be such that one layout leads easily to the other. Fig. 2.4 shows three possible layouts for multiple control systems involving sequential operation. In each case a meter and related control, assumed to be continuously used, are given a dominant location and would be in the most convenient viewing and controlling position.

Where controls and displays are used in a more random manner, layout should be based upon the following aspects:

1. Display and control importance for safety and efficient operation.
2. Frequency of use. More frequently used controls and displays being more convenient to the operator than those less frequently used.
3. Grouping of controls and displays which perform a common service.

Displays and controls on a car facia provide a useful example here. In the majority of cars, the facia controls include ignition, choke,

c

lights, windscreen wiper, windscreen washer, heater controls, speedometer and oil temperature gauge. Speedometer, lights, wiper and
washer are important for safe and efficient operation. In addition they
are likely to be the most frequently used. Consequently they should
be most convenient to the driver. The remaining controls would
occupy a secondary position but, since some are interrelated or provide
a common service, they would be grouped together. Thus ignition
and choke could be located adjacent to each other while heater and
possibly ventilator controls would form another group.

In many devices, as with the car, displays and controls can be
grouped when each group performs a distinct task within the whole
task. If a number of groups involve sequential operation then it is
preferable to employ similar sequential patterns. It is particularly

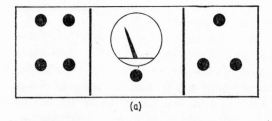

(a)

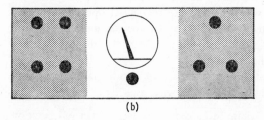

(b)

FIG. 2.5 *Methods of defining
groups of controls on panels*
(a) *By lines*
(b) *By changes of panel tone
  or colour*
(c) *By using mimic systems
  Arrangements (a) and
(b) are more suitable for test
instruments, while arrangement (c) is more suitable for
control panels such as those
of electrical or chemical control stations.*

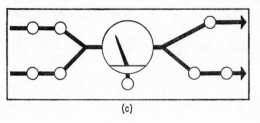

(c)

important to define each group possibly as shown in Fig. 2.5. If importance and frequency of use are the determining factors then group layout will depend upon placing the most important and the most frequently used groups in positions which are most convenient to the operator. The layout in an aircraft control cabin is one such example.

2.3 SUMMARY ON THE GENERAL APPROACH TO MAN/MACHINE RELATIONSHIPS

By keeping the control loop principle in mind when studying any particular control action there is less likelihood that significant factors are overlooked. Further by using the six features of the loop to make column headings, a list describing the main features involved throughout a complete task can be compiled. Part of such a list referring to a bench drill task is shown in Table 2.1 p. 36. It is important to compile the list from the very beginning to the absolute completion of any task. When the list comes to be used for design purposes the location of any product feature can then be judged against *all* the activities in which the feature may be involved. For example, when designing a centre-lathe, it would be tempting to locate the centres at a position which would allow for most convenient viewing. However a complete task analysis undertaken in tabular form immediately shows that centre location will also depend upon loading, measuring and unloading the work being machined. In the case of general purpose machines such as centre lathes, it will be necessary to undertake several analyses according to the variety of tasks envisaged. It will also be necessary to assess how frequently different types of task will be performed. From such investigations, display and control features can be arranged to suit the task which is likely to be most frequently undertaken, provided other tasks do not make any special demands upon the operator.

While it may be comparatively easy to describe the main features in any control loop, such a description will not lead automatically to selection of the best possible displays or controls. In criticising the traditional micrometer it was pointed out that a numeral reading would be easier to appreciate than a scalar reading which involves some computation. However, in the speed control example, Fig. 2.1, it may not be assumed that a numeral indicator is necessarily the most

Table 2.1. PART OF AN OPERATOR'S CHART FOR A DRILLING TASK USING CONTROL LOOP ELEMENTS AS TABLE HEADINGS; ALSO SUGGESTING QUESTIONS WHICH MIGHT BE ASKED WHEN CONSIDERING EACH OPERATION

Task	Principal Display	MAN Principal Input	MAN Principal Output	Principal Control	Possible Factors Needing Examination
Mount workpiece	Workpiece Drill table Clamps	Eyes	Hands	Drill table clamps	Is table height convenient to hands and sight? Are clamps easily fitted?
Mount drill	Drill chuck and key	Eyes Hands	Hands	Chuck and key	Is chuck convenient to hands and sight?
Set drill depth	Drawing Drill depth indicator	Eyes	Hands	Depth indicator stop	Is depth indicator clearly visible?
Set drill speed	Speed tables Belt or gear change unit	Eyes	Hands	Speed change system	Can change system be easily operated without relying on memory or disturbing guards?
Check guards in position	Guard locking system	Eyes Hands	Hands	Guard locking system	Is guard safety interlock adequate?
Centre workpiece	Workpiece Drill tip	Eyes	Hands	Drill table clamps	Is lighting adequate for centring purposes?
Switch Drill main switch	Main switch	Eyes	Hands	Main switch	Is switch convenient? Does it clearly show 'on' and 'off'
Drill	On-off button Operating lever Workpiece Drill tip	Eyes Hands	Hands	On-off button Operating lever	Is on-off button to hand? Is lever convenient—able to 'feel' drill—moving in expected direction?

suitable. In this situation the operator may not only need to know the speed but also the rate of change of speed. A numeral indicator would not show rate of change so clearly as the movement of a pointer against a scale. Consequently the latter may be preferred. But should the operator need to record speed, say on a log sheet, a scalar indicator might well be augmented by a numeral indicator, possibly with a 'dwell' system should the speed be subject to fairly rapid variations. Thus it is always necessary to ensure that the operator is receiving information in a form which requires the least amount of interpretation.

A complete task analysis and a thorough appraisal of each individual control action should, in general, precede the search for data from those textbooks which are available on ergonomics. It is then more likely that the data, which may have been developed from one set of circumstances, will not be applied blindly to the equipment under study.

Finally, while a designer can and should be concerned with all the physical factors which may interrupt, restrict or distort the flow of information in each control loop, there are some factors with which he may not be able to cope in his design. However, there is every reason for giving guidance on how the machine should be set up so that its operator can function in the most efficient manner. For example, if the operator has to examine work of a highly polished nature, the designer may specify that directional lighting, likely to induce specular glare from the work, should be avoided. The engineering designer usually specifies requirements for optimum technical performance and machine maintenance, so he should also include requirements for optimum operator performance both in relation to his machine and to its envisaged physical environment. It should be remembered that, at base, the efficiency of any machine depends not only upon its own efficiency but upon that of the man/machine combination.

2.4 MAN IN THE CONTROL LOOP

Unfortunately, at least from the designer's viewpoint when he comes to locate controls and displays in relation to the operator, there is no such person as the average man. The designer has to cater for variations in body height, eye level height, arm reach and so on. There will also be differences in muscular ability, sensory perception and reaction time. Furthermore in some circumstances differences of temperament may influence effiicent operation. In this case the problem may become one of fitting man to the machine by personnel selection, as is the case with aircraft pilots. In some circumstances the nature of the task will demand a fairly rigid specification of human abilities, as is the case with space-pilots, but in by far the majority of cases equipment has to be designed to suit a wide variety of people; in many instances both male and female and of different nationalities. If a product is to be used by men and women in say Japan and the U.S.A. then clearly the designer is faced with having to suit people with considerable differences in height. He will also need to take account of cultural differences, the most obvious one being language which may influence identification and instruction lettering. Should he prefer to use symbols in order to avoid language variations then it will be necessary to ensure that these symbols are readily understood.

Fortunately, when considering body dimensions, a degree of order can be given to values which at first sight may appear to be quite random in character. By taking measurements of a large number of people it has been found that dimensional variations can fall along a hump-backed curve known to statisticians as a curve of normal distribution or Gaussian curve. Such a curve for height variation is shown in Fig. 2.6. This curve shows that very few subjects are extremely short or extremely tall while the majority of people cluster around the arithmetic mean. It is clear from the symmetrical form of the curve, that half the measured population are shorter than the mean value and half are taller.

Given two values, namely the arithmetic mean and the 'standard deviation', a number of characteristics can be deduced from a curve of normal distribution. The arithmetic mean is readily understood and may be expressed as follows.

$$\text{arithmetic mean } H = \frac{\Sigma h}{n}$$

where n = number of measurements

The standard deviation describes the manner in which variations fall about the mean. It is equal to the square root of the mean of the sum of the squares of all the differences between the arithmetic mean and each individual measurement.

$$\text{Thus standard deviation } (\sigma) = \sqrt{\frac{\Sigma\,(H-h)^2}{n}}$$

The standard deviation is used as follows. For all practical purposes it can be said that 34% of a measured group will lie one standard

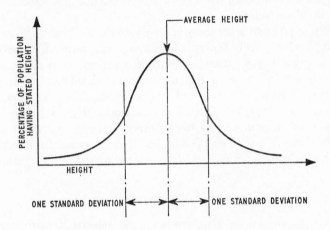

FIG. 2.6 *Body dimensions, such as height, for a measured population follow a curve o fnormal distribution or Gaussian curve*

deviation (i.e. $1 \times \sigma$) below the mean and one standard deviation above the mean. Thus 68% of the measured group are covered by one standard deviation. In a similar way, approximately 95% are covered by two standard deviations and 99% by three standard deviations. For example, the mean height of male personnel in the Royal Navy was found to be 68·1 in and the standard deviation calculated to be 2·31 in. Thus 68% of personnel fell within the range 68·1 + 2·31 and 68·1 − 2·31; or 70·4 in and 65·8 in respectively. It may be found that 95% fell within the range 63·5–72·7 in, and 99% within the range 61·2–75·0 in.

Comprehensive tables of anthropometric data should always quote standard deviations together with mean values so that the designer may assess variations from the mean for different percentages of the measured population. It is most unlikely that he will need to cater for all the population for, as the curve of normal distribution shows, extreme cases, whether in height or any other characteristic, will be rare. A 90% range will usually cope with most practical requirements. This means that the designer is selecting a range 45% below the mean and 45% above the mean, excluding 5% at one extreme and 5% at the other. A 90% range is obtained by multiplying the standard deviation by 1·65 and making the appropriate subtraction from and addition to the mean value.

Some tables of anthropometric data do quote either 90%, or 95% ranges. Occasionally however 'percentiles' are specified. A percentile is simply a measure at or below which a percentage of the measured group will fall. Suppose that the maximum height of all the R.N. personnel who were measured was 80 in, then 80 in represents the hundredth percentile since all the measured subjects had or were below this height. Clearly the arithmetic mean is equivalent to the fiftieth percentile and selection of a 90% range means that dimensions are being chosen between the fifth and the ninety-fifth percentile.

2.5 USING ANTHROPOMETRIC DATA

Body dimensions are recorded for nude subjects in fairly upright postures, that is without stoop or appreciable deflection of the main limb joints. Consequently due account must be taken of clothing and of more natural stances. For example most people tend to look along a line about 3° below the horizontal, further they do not adopt rigidly erect positions. Clothing may make an appreciable difference. On average, shoes will change a man's height by about an inch while height changes for women may be appreciable. Headgear can influence door heights, while body clothing will affect access or passage ways. Gloves and shoes may affect the size and placement of hand and foot controls so that they can be easily operated and given sufficient clearance from other controls and machine features.

During the course of design work, by far the best approach to using anthropometric data is made by constructing two-dimensional manikins preferably of front and side elevations of the human figure. These manikins should be constructed from available data concerning those for whom the product is intended. Ideally three sizes for each elevation should be constructed; one for the lowest selected per-centile measurement, one for the mean measurement and one for the highest percentile. Making due allowance for clothing and stance, an assessment of control convenience can then be made. If manikins are only constructed for the so-called average man then errors may easily be encouraged. If a control panel is located at arm's reach for the average man, clearly it will be inconvenient for those with less than average arm length. Equally a close clearance door height for the average man will produce difficulties for all those who are taller than the average. By using three manikins, errors of this kind can be largely avoided.

2.6 LIMITATIONS OF ANTHROPOMETRIC DATA

Perhaps the first limitation is that the designer cannot always obtain full data regarding those who will use his equipment. He may be forced to make assumptions. One such assumption, adequate for general use though not precisely correct, may be to take it that the proportions of the human body are similar for similar age groups. Clearly the proportions of children are different from those of adults. But, given one dimension such as stature for any particular group, other dimensions can be arranged by proportional relationships with groups which have been (more thoroughly) studied. Another limitation is that data may tend to lose its authenticity over a period of time. For example, it is well known that, in the last twenty years, children have increased in stature. Another difficulty may be that if a clearly defined group is being considered then any changes in definition may affect the data. For example if all members in a group were required to be 6 ft tall or taller then a considerable change would occur if the height requirement were changed to 5 ft 9 in.

Finally, the most important limitation is that most anthropometric data give no indication of the arcs of movement of which the human frame is capable. Even where such information has been produced it is usually based upon locating arcs from points considered to be centres of movement. But human beings are not pin-jointed. Their movements are fairly complex and often involve the whole body structure. Consequently, while anthropometric data and pin-jointed manikins are valuable for preliminary design assessments, checks with live subjects should be made in the design stages as soon as possible. The crudest of mock-ups can be of considerable value in assuring that controls and displays are conveniently located. *Live* checks should be made with at least three subjects corresponding to the lowest considered percentile, three subjects around the arithmetic mean and three at the highest percentile. It is also useful to check that the subjects do not differ to any great extent from those they are intended to represent. For example, if they all happened to be left-handed, then they would not truly represent a population likely to be predominantly right-handed. In addition their performance should be carefully watched over several trials. Finally the designer should exclude himself from any test group. The performance of a test group should be watched from the very beginning to the absolute completion of the task. So-called spot checks of the convenience of one particular control, even one having a dominant role, are not as effective as if considered in relation to the operation of other controls.

In many situations components such as levers, handwheels, handles and seats may require more thorough examination and with a larger number of test subjects. This will be especially so either where force must be exerted or where, as with a tractor or truck seats, the operator will use the component for some time. Since in such a case it may be difficult and probably misleading to simulate conditions involving forces such as vibrations and accelerations (liable to influence tractor seat design), tests may not be possible until an experimental version of the product has been built.

2.7 CONCLUSIONS

This brief survey of ergonomics must be supplemented by studying those text books which now exist on the subject and which are noted in the Bibliography. Ergonomics is a subject which both engineering and industrial designers should study closely for on the one hand it will influence the engineer's choice of mechanisms, while on the other hand it will affect the industrial designer's approach to visual aspects. With this in mind, an approach to the visual effects of line and form can now be made.

Chapter Three

VISUAL EFFECTS OF
LINE AND FORM

THE sense of sight is man's major means of forming impressions of the
world around him. Whether considered from ergonomic or aesthetic
standpoints, the amount of information which can be received by way
of the eyes, and the ability to sort out and give meaning to this
information, is of considerable importance. It can easily be shown
that what is 'seen' is not always 'there', conversely what is 'there' is
not always 'seen'. The optical illusions in Fig. 3.1 may go some way
towards making this clear. Seeing is a complex activity which, purely
for purposes of examination, can be considered in two parts. There
is the way the eyes function as mechanisms for transferring information
to the brain, and there is the way the brain interprets and acts upon this
information. It is proposed to examine the effect of line and form in
relation to these two aspects, and then to assess their influence upon
reactions to features in engineering products.

3.1 THE MECHANICS OF SEEING

The eye is usually compared with a camera because, as with a camera,
it possesses an iris to control the amount of light entering it and a
lens for focusing an image onto a screen. However, apart from these
similarities, there is little else which can be compared. The main
features in the eye are shown in Fig. 3.2. Light enters the protective
cornea and reaches the lens by way of a transparent fluid, the aqueous

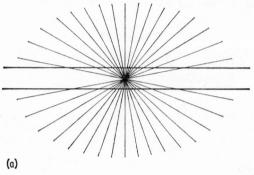

(a)

FIG. 3.1 *What is seen is not always 'there' i.e. in (a) the heavy lines seen as curved are in fact parallel. Conversely what is 'there' is not always seen i.e. in (b) a redundancy occurs*

(b)

humour, and the pupil which is the central aperture in the iris. The pupil closes in bright light and opens in dim light, as does the aperture in a camera. But the method of operation is quite different; the eye's iris being operated by a muscle having a circular and radial action. The lens is focused not by moving it backwards and forwards as in a camera, but by changing its shape. This is carried out by the ciliary muscle located around the lens. From the lens, the light passes through the vitreous humour, which maintains the shape of the eyeball, and then impinges upon the retina, the sensitive wall at the rear of the eye.

The retina is composed of two kinds of light-sensitive cell namely rods and cones. The approximate distribution of these cells is shown in Fig. 3.2 (a). They are connected by nerve fibres to the optic nerve and hence to the brain. The place where the optic nerve leaves the eye is known as the blind spot, being in fact a small region in which there is no sensitivity. The rods and cones have distinctly different functions. The cones are most concentrated at the fovea, the region which gives the clearest vision under normal illumination such as daylight. The cones also enable colour perception. They thin out from the fovea and their place is taken by the rods which, as described in Section 4.3, cannot detect colour. The rods are effective for night vision when the cones become inoperative. They also enable the detection of motion. Other features of the eye's structure are the choroid coat, a dark layer backing the retina to eliminate reflections, the sclerotic coat which provides a

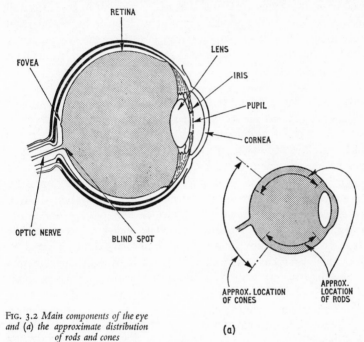

FIG. 3.2 *Main components of the eye and (a) the approximate distribution of rods and cones*

(a)

protective outer layer and the conjunctiva which screens the front of the eyeball adjacent to the cornea.

The eyes of the average adult are spaced roughly 2 ins apart and this causes each eye to send a different pattern of signals to the brain; a difference which helps in the perception of depth and distance. When concentrating upon an object, the eyes are constantly moving with a very small but rapid action. This action is necessary for clear vision and can be appreciated if an effort is made to look with a fixed stare at any object. It will become indistinct very quickly. While these minute movements are necessary for concentrated vision, the eyes have several characteristic actions for different types of observation. The saccadic eye movement is simply a series of jumps from one fixation to another and can be noticed by watching someone reading a book. The pursuit movement, as the expression implies, refers to steady movement noticeable in a person watching an object in motion. The nystagmoid movement identifies a sharp movement in one direction coupled with a slower return movement. It may be observed in someone watching telegraph poles from a car. Here the eyes are likely to pick up and follow a pole until it passes and then flick to the next pole along the route.

As with other human qualities and abilities there are differences in visual abilities. Apart from the incidence of colour blindness, mentioned in Section 4.3.2, and variations in dark adaptation (the ability to see at very low levels of illumination), there are two main characteristics which can influence reactions to line and form. The ability to focus from near to distant objects, by changing the shape of the lens is known as Accommodation. In normal vision the eye accommodates over a focal distance of from about 10 in to 20 ft. No accommodation takes place over approximately 20 ft which may be regarded in the photographic sense as optical infinity. The ability to accommodate may not only vary from person to person but may also be affected by age. A child can focus on objects as close as 3 in from the eyes whereas by the age of twenty it may be difficult to focus on objects at about 6 in from the eyes. This is because, with increasing age, the lens tends to lose its flexibility. Short-sighted people are those whose minimum focal distance is less than about 10 in but who cannot clearly see objects at a distance. Long-sighted people are those who can see objects at a distance but their minimum focal distance is greater than the approximate figure of 10 in.

The ability to perceive detail is known as Acuity. Apart from variations from one person to another, acuity is mainly affected by the level of prevailing illumination and the amount of light reflected from the perceived detail in relation to the amount of light reflected from its background. This latter factor is usually called Brightness

Ratio. Up to levels of illumination well beyond those likely to be met in normal circumstances, acuity increases with increasing illumination. It also increases as the brightness ratio increases. Thus where detail and background are not in themselves illuminants, the greatest brightness ratio could be obtained either by placing black features on a white background or white features on a black background. Acuity can be assessed in a variety of ways, one of which is shown in Fig. 3.3. This illustration shows that detail, here the gap between the black bars is less easily perceived as the brightness ratio is reduced.

Though acuity increases with an increase in illumination, disturbing influences can arise mainly from two effects. The Brightness Ratio refers to the perceived detail and its *immediate* background. If the general background is either very much darker or, more important, very much lighter than the detail and its immediate background, acuity can be impaired. It can also be influenced by the presence of brighter features which, while coming into the visual field, are not part of those features under concentrated examination. These features may be either light sources giving rise to direct glare or light-reflecting

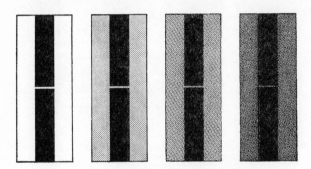

FIG. 3.3 *Visual acuity decreases as the Brightness Ratio (i.e. contrast between perceived detail and immediate background) decreases*

features giving rise to reflected glare. Fig. 3.4 (*a*) shows an example of a situation in which these effects may combine to reduce the ability to read a conventional dial gauge. These may be related with the phototropic effect which describes the tendency for the eyes to be drawn to the brightest feature in any visual field; this is described in Section 4.7. The phototropic effect may be most noticeable at night

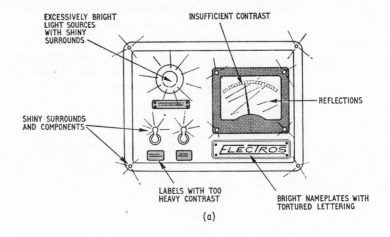

EXCESSIVELY BRIGHT
LIGHT SOURCES
WITH SHINY
SURROUNDS

INSUFFICIENT CONTRAST

REFLECTIONS

SHINY SURROUNDS
AND COMPONENTS

LABELS WITH TOO
HEAVY CONTRAST

BRIGHT NAMEPLATES WITH
TORTURED LETTERING

(a)

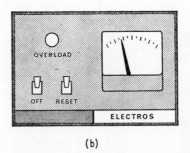

(b)

Fig. 3.4 *While increased illumination improves acuity, the factors shown in (a) would in general,
oppose this improvement. (b) shows a more appropriate arrangement*

when some effort may be required to prevent the eyes being drawn
to street lights or the headlights of approaching traffic. Fig. 3.4 (*b*)
shows an approximate light distribution which would overcome faults
in Fig. 3.4 (*a*). It may be noted that while black on white features have
been chosen for the dial gauge (giving maximum Brightness Ratio),
white on black features might possibly be used. However above a
certain level of illumination giving a reflectance of about 10 ft. L,
white features may tend to blur.

While, with the eyes looking straight ahead, the visual field is

(a)

(Photograph by courtesy of Race Furniture
Ltd., London, S.W.4. & C.o.I.D., London,
S.W.1.)

(b)

(Photograph by courtesy of Kandya Ltd.,
Hayes, Middlesex)

PLATE 3.1 *Visual impressions may not be supported by fact. For example the rod framed
chair (a), though appearing lighter, is heavier than the wooden chair (b)*

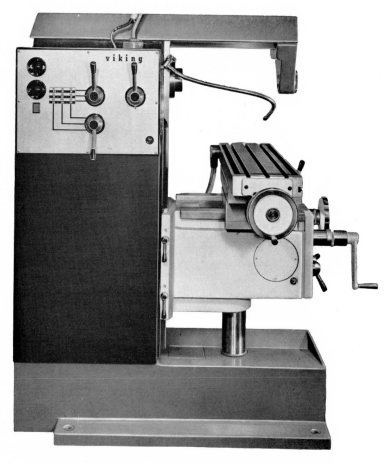

PLATE 4.1 *Paint scheme for a small milling machine. Note the clarity of control area both in being immediately seen and in relation to layout. Maker: Mondiale. Consultant industrial designers: Société Technès*
(Photograph by courtesy of S.P.R.L. Bauteurs, Bruxelles)

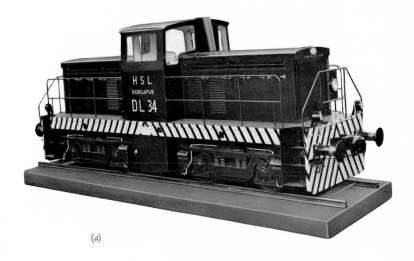

(a)

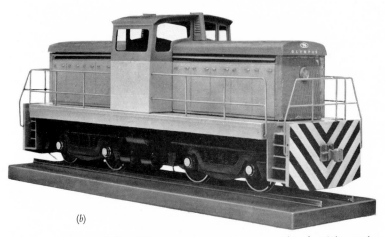

(b)

PLATE 4.2 *Paint scheme in (a), all black to customer's order destroys machine form (Photograph: Hallowes & Johnston, Sheffield 11). The consultant's recommendations, on the model in (b) help define and co-ordinate the major features of the locomotive (Photograph: J. S. Markiewicz, London, S.W.12). Maker: Yorkshire Engine Co. Consultant industrial designer: F. C. Ashford*

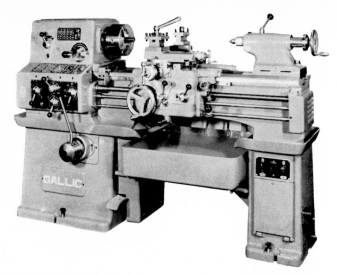

(a) 'Gallic' lathe before being re-designed
(Photograph: Société Mondiale, Belgium)

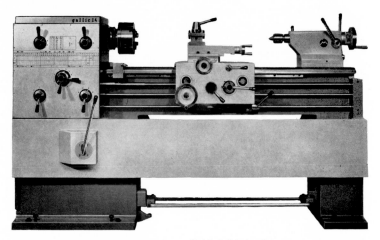

(b) 'Gallic' lathe after re-designing
(Photograph: S.P.R.L. Bauteurs)

PLATE 5.1 *Removal of 'visual clutter' and clarification of main features of this lathe help to give a clearer impression of an efficient machine. Maker: Mondiale. Consultant industrial designer: Société Technès*

bounded roughly by the axes shown in Fig. 3.5, the region over which clear vision is obtained is extremely small, something like a tenth of an inch at minimum focal distances. This can be confirmed by concentrating on any particular feature. It will be found that unless the eyes are moved, adjacent features are blurred. It must be admitted however, that it is difficult to prevent the eyes from moving to adjacent detail particularly if, as with concentrating on a letter in a word, the adjacent features have a related meaning. It is this small area of clear vision which necessitates the characteristic movements mentioned earlier. Although not consciously realised, sharpness of perception decreases towards the outer edges of the visual field and colour perception also deteriorates. These variations of perception in the visual field are determined by the size of the fovea, the most sensitive

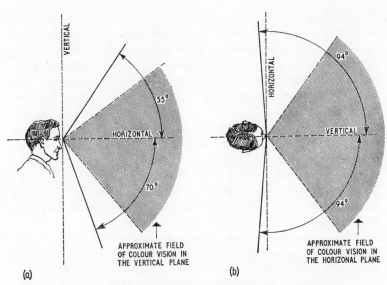

FIG. 3.5 *Approximate field of vision with the eyes fixed on a point*

region under normal illumination and by the replacement of the cones by rods towards the outer edges of the retina. When the cones become inoperative in the dark, clarity of perception depends upon the rods. At night, a feature is most clearly seen by looking at it obliquely.

Before leaving the mechanics of seeing two other visual character-

D

istics may be noted, one of which is considered more fully in Section 4.3.1. This is the influence of 'after-image' which describes the retention of impressions after the eyes have looked away from a subject under fairly concentrated survey. It is quite possible that after-images are constantly occurring but that they are not consciously recognised. Where so-called negative after-images occur as described in Section 4.3.1, their effect can be more readily recognised and may on occasions be disturbing. Finally, visual images are retained for around one twentieth of a second; a characteristic which gives rise to the impression of motion gained in the cinema where, in fact, the eyes are being presented with a series of 'stills'.

3.2 THE PSYCHOLOGY OF SEEING

The signals sent to the brain along the optic nerve do not reproduce the retinal image in the brain as, for example, the signals from a television transmitter produce a picture on a television receiver. All that can be said is that the brain is stimulated by the signals it receives and gives meaning to this stimulus from acquired experience. In the very early formative years, a baby may react to a bright light by blinking or his eyes may be seen to follow a moving object. But the shape of the light or moving object and their location in space is probably not realised until the baby is at least a year old. He will reach for objects beyond his grasp and may well pay no attention to an object seen from a different position than that which may be familiar. In her book *The Psychology of Perception*, Professor Vernon says, 'Thus until about the ninth month, if the baby's bottle is given him with the nipple turned away from him he makes no attempt to grasp it as he would if the nipple were turned towards him. Its appearance in the former position is so different from that in the latter that he does not recognise it as his bottle.'

The infant learns by a combination of touch and sight until he has produced a mental concept, say of a table, so that by the time he is a year old some objects may be recognisable though they look different when viewed from different angles and at different distances. From then on, the ability to discriminate between objects begins to develop with the natural exploratory nature of the child. But it may take some time before, for example, all four-legged animals are not labelled as 'dogs'. Here obviously some account must be taken of limitations in vocabulary. Even so, the recognition of objects as a learned experience can be recognised from everyday behaviour. For example, those who are not particularly interested in cars cannot differentiate between different types by comparison with those who are car enthusiasts. The latter may be able to identify even an uncommon vehicle with apparently the briefest of glances.

When objects are viewed they appear sharp and clear partly because from experience it is known that they possess form and substance, partly due to stereoscopic vision and partly because of the Brightness Ratio between the contour of the object and its background. When attention is either directed to or attracted by any feature in the visual field this feature tends to become 'real' while all other features lose significance. This is called the 'figure on ground' effect and is fundamental to the perception and recognition of features. In Fig. 3.6 (a) the small square will always become figural against the ground of the large square. However if the square is enlarged as in Fig. 3.6 (b) it may not be so readily seen as a black figure on a white ground so much as a white figure surrounding a black ground. The optical illusion in Fig. 3.6 (c) is often used to show that when the areas are

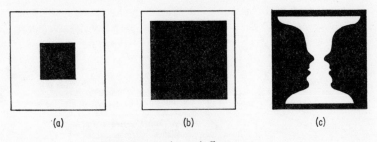

(a)   (b)   (c)

FIG. 3.6 Figure and ground effects
(a) the black square is seen as the figure
(b) the white surround is liable to become figural
(c) alternation between figure and ground occurs

roughly similar, alternation may occur. Thus, it is likely that at first sight the observer will see a white goblet against a black ground. Indeed this impression may persist for some time until, and perhaps suddenly, two human profiles are seen facing each other. It may be noted that in either case the ground tends to lose its identity. When the goblet is being seen the black areas seem to recede and when the two faces are noticed the white area loses its significance.

While the identification of features depends upon their Brightness Ratio in relation to other features, it also depends upon whether they are regarded as having any significance. The German Gestalt psycho-

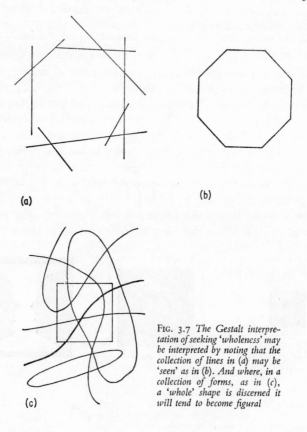

(a)

(b)

(c)

FIG. 3.7 *The Gestalt interpretation of seeking 'wholeness' may be interpreted by noting that the collection of lines in (a) may be 'seen' as in (b). And where, in a collection of forms, as in (c), a 'whole' shape is discerned it will tend to become figural*

logists (Gestalt means form), proposed that objects or features become significant when they demonstrate a 'whole' quality and that perception is, in fact, 'whole-seeking'. The meaning of this may become apparent in Fig. 3.7 (*a*). Here the lines will be seen as a collection forming a 'whole' shape probably as shown in Fig. 3.7 (*b*). The observer will tend to regularise and simplify the shape eliminating 'superfluities'. Consequently when presented with a collection of features such as shown in Fig. 3.7 (c) he may readily pick out the square as figure regarding the remainder as ground. The simplicity and regularity of the square is regarded as 'whole'. Indeed this whole-seeking tendency may produce wholes when they do not, in fact, exist. Thus the spots in Fig. 3.8 (a) are regarded as forming the corners of a square, while those in Fig. 3.8 (b) are regarded as forming an incomplete hexagon. The identification of 'wholeness' is strongly influenced by simplicity and regularity. The mind is, as it were, pattern seeking, and as seen from the spots, may well create a pattern image which it imposes upon reality. Thus the shapes in Fig. 3.8 (c) and 3.8 (d) may in fact be seen respectively as a square and a circle.

Features of similar form may also be 'seen as one'. Thus in Fig. 3.9 (a); the diagrammatic dial gauges will be seen as one group while the symbolised control knobs will be seen as another. Proximity of features also influences the 'wholeness' with which they are regarded. Thus, in Fig. 3.9 (b), an observer will tend to see three groups of dials rather than six dials. These tendencies are clearly of considerable value in laying out features, say on a control panel, so that they can be readily

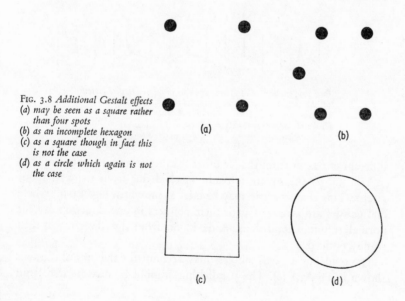

FIG. 3.8 *Additional Gestalt effects*
(a) *may be seen as a square rather than four spots*
(b) *as an incomplete hexagon*
(c) *as a square though in fact this is not the case*
(d) *as a circle which again is not the case*

(a)

(b)

(c)

(d)

identified; although as pointed out in Section 2.2, this should be done to suit operating requirements and not to satisfy some quite arbitrary pattern-seeking tendency.

The appeal of 'wholeness' may be regarded in another way by noticing that a feature will readily become figural when it has a

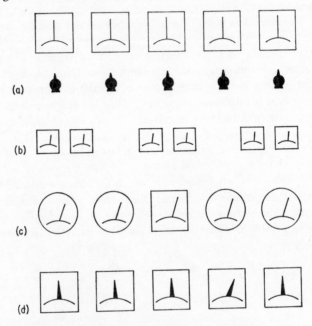

FIG. 3.9 *Application of Gestalt concepts to control feature layouts*
(a) *the dials are seen as one group and the knobs as another*
(b) *three pairs of dials are seen rather than six dials*
(c) *the square dial is readily picked out*
(d) *deviation from 'normal' in one dial gauge is readily detected*

different character from that of other features forming a pattern. Thus in Fig. 3.9 (c) the square is readily picked out from the pattern of circles. This characteristic may be used as shown in Fig. 3.9 (d) where dial gauges are arranged with their pointers in one direction say for normal running conditions. A deviation from this direction is then readily noticed.

The tendency to see 'wholes' may account for the optical illusions shown in Fig. 3.1 (a). The parallel lines cannot be disassociated from the radial lines in the circle. They appear convex because there is too strong a tendency to see the illustration as a whole. In short, attempts to make the parallel lines figural are foiled by the dominance of the other lines.

The foregoing aspects of perception undoubtedly play a large part in determining reactions to composite forms. Indeed, it is tempting to relate the Gestalt concept of 'wholeness' to the concept of 'unity' introduced in Chapter Five. The tendency to seek pattern might also be related to the concept of order also introduced in Chapter Five. However there is one more, and especially important, aspect of perception which bears upon reactions to line and form. This is the tendency to ascribe meaning to perceived features. The simple form in Fig. 3.10 (a) may make this plain. One observer may see it as the

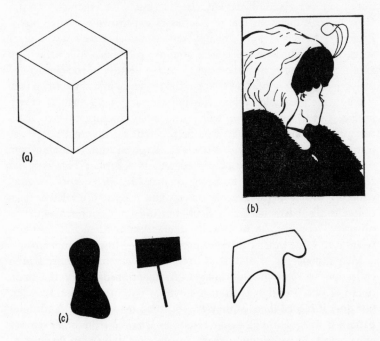

FIG. 3.10 *Different meanings can be given to perceived features for example in (a) the observer may see a cube, the interior of a three sided enclosure or a hexagon divided in three, in (b) constant examination produces quite a different meaning, in (c) different meanings will be given to these shapes by different observers*

representation of a cube, another as the inside of a three-sided structure; a third may see it as a hexagon partitioned by a tripodal frame. One sees what one wants to see; a fact which may be demonstrated by the startling illustration Fig. 3.10 (b), shown by C. J. Adcock in his book, *Fundamentals of Psychology*. Here, there is no doubt about which is figure and which is background with regard to the illustration as a whole. But constant study of this illustration will produce an extraordinary metamorphosis. An interesting point is that when this change occurs (and in some people this may take time), it occurs in an instant. One moment the picture has one meaning, the next it has quite a different meaning.

The desire to give meaning to perceived objects undoubtedly comes from the whole process of learning to see in which, as pointed out earlier, perceived objects are related to established mental concepts. C. J. Adcock mentions one of a series of experiments, carried out at Princeton University, in which observers thought they saw a chair when looking through a peephole at a group of lines. But seen from another angle the chair turned out to be a collection of rods suspended in space and only appearing to form the structure of a chair when seen through the peephole. When viewing abstract shapes such as shown in Fig. 3.10 (c) an observer will immediately attempt to give them meaning and meanings may well be different for different people. A feature in a visual field which tends to be given more meaning than other features will readily be picked out. In Chapters Five and Six reference is made to the tendency to establish 'stereotypes'; mental concepts with which perceived objects and features are related. If an object is alleged to be say, a chair, but does not conform with the observer's concept, he may well either reject it as such or perhaps relate it to some other concept which, to him, is more comparable.

Mental concepts of perceived objects are very much more than a collection of photographic images. As mentioned earlier the brain does not interpret signals from the eyes as with a television receiver, nor does it record them as they are recorded by a camera. A stimulus pattern is set up and will evoke responses acquired from other sensory experiences. In perceiving a chair, an observer will assign qualities of solidity and strength to it from his experience of handling and sitting in chairs. It will appear hard or soft, heavy or light, stable or unstable according to his experiences. But these sensations are clearly not confined solely to experiences of chairs, relationships are made with other forms having similar apparent hardness, softness, weight and so on. For example, not long after the Second World War there was a mild fashion for chairs made in steel rod. An example is shown in Plate 3.1 by comparison with a chair having a moulded plywood seat. The steel chair appears to be lighter partly because less volume of material is used and partly because the mind relates it to other frame structures which are believed to be or are in fact lighter than equivalent and more solid structures. In fact, because of relative material densities, the steel chair is distinctly heavier than the wooden chair.

When these chairs first appeared, they were rejected by some people because they did not conform with concepts built up from prior experience. Even now they may 'look wrong' while other chairs may 'look right'. Thus when engineers who like to use these expressions say that a product 'looks right', they should pause to consider whether they are making this statement entirely from collective experience or whether it derives from an examination which confirms that the product's form is precisely tailored to its function. Of course, in practice the engineer's experience, built up from technical knowledge, may very well produce an accurate assessment. But there can be no certainty of this unless it is backed by a sound technical appraisal. Since, as pointed out in Section 1.2, the form of many products can be manipulated without influencing technical or even ergonomic requirements, such products cannot be judged in terms of 'rightness' or 'wrongness' as might be the case with products whose function is strongly dependent upon their external form, e.g. aircraft. Thus in so far as one may be concerned with producing a visual expression of a product's function (and this as shown in Chapter Four is certainly not the only criterion for judging form), the concern is not with 'wrongness' or 'rightness' but, as expressed by F. C. Ashford, with suitability or non-suitability. Judgement as to whether a form is suitable or not will be very strongly determined by the vast range of concepts and associated experiences which have been built up. The engineer may have, as it were, an informed experience but other people will share his experience though they may not have his technical knowledge. Thus almost everyone would find a column which tapers in towards the base somewhat startling because experience of all columnar features has been that they do not normally possess this characteristic. And they

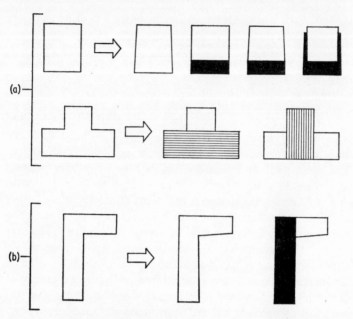

FIG. 3.11 *Stability can be expressed by (a) giving more apparent mass to the base of structures or by (b) emphasising the supporting structures. Note the difference between the inverted T structures though they are similar in overall dimensions*

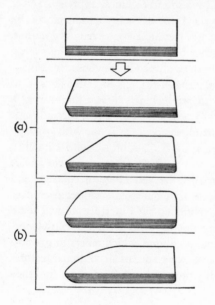

FIG. 3.12 *Mobility can be expressed by (a) using diagonals to give a directional effect, or by (b) using flowing forms Both are used, often excessively in car design and copy aerodynamic forms*

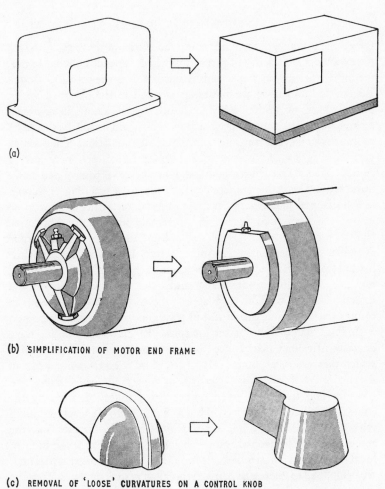

(a)

(b) SIMPLIFICATION OF MOTOR END FRAME

(c) REMOVAL OF 'LOOSE' CURVATURES ON A CONTROL KNOB

FIG. 3.13 *Precision is a more subtle characteristic. It is partly expressed by clearly defined contours as in (a) by the removal of protuberances as in (b) and by careful attention to details as in (c)*

will have this experience though they lack even a rudimentary knowledge of the theory of structures.

3.3 GENERAL INFLUENCES OF LINE AND FORM

Reactions to line and form are compounded from the ways in which the eyes work, the clarity of perception which depends upon more than the eye's efficiency as a mechanism and involves the so-called Gestalt aspects, and also upon the meanings ascribed to the observed forms. In his lectures on aesthetics F. C. Ashford describes how, in combination, these aspects can produce reactions which will usually be shared by most people. By rendering down forms into combinations of horizontal, vertical, diagonal and curved lines, he shows that each may have a certain effect. Thus horizontals tend to create a passive and stable impression. This is due perhaps partly to the easier scanning of features in a horizontal plane, partly because objects are usually located in, as it were, a horizontal world and partly because many horizontal features for example, flat stretches of land and the horizon, are regarded as stable. A vertical line seems more active. It tends to interrupt the natural scanning action and thus becomes more significant. A diagonal line may seem even more active and tends to express motion and direction. A sinuous line may appear the most pronounced both in terms of attracting attention and in giving an impression of mobility.

As F. C. Ashford shows, the interplay of forms incorporating these characteristic lines does much to determine reactions to objects in which they are incorporated. However, it must be recognised that in the majority of cases the 'lines' of an object are really edges and contours and that their visual influence is strongly dictated by the context in which they are seen. Thus as F. C. Ashford shows in dealing with the 'lines' of a train, a removal of vertical features and the accentuation of horizontal features helps to produce an impression of motion, albeit in a horizontal direction. But in this context horizontals are being used to express dynamic rather than passive qualities. Thus the diagonal lines of an arrow or the use of diagonals to express motion do not have the same effect as when seen in, say, the Pyramids of Egypt, which express a massive stability. Similarly while curved forms may be used to express mobility they can also evoke impressions of gentleness and be regarded as more 'sympathetic' than angular forms.

It must be emphasised therefore, that the effects shown in Figs. 3.11, 3.12 and 3.13 may not always apply. A very great deal depends upon the meanings ascribed to them when they are seen in relation to the function of the object and in relation to the environment. In addition while everyone has acquired a large measure of common experience, that is they will tend to see things in the same way, there are bound to be some differences depending upon the nature of each person's prior experience. However, while making these qualifications, it will be seen that comparatively mild structural changes can produce distinctly different impressions. This fact is often overlooked by engineers to whom a row of bolts or a nameplate may seem unimportant because they may perform comparatively minor functional roles. But in visual terms such features may well destroy whatever impression is required. Clearly the effects shown in Figs. 3.11 to 3.13 can be augmented or destroyed by the way in which colour is used. Colour is integral with all visual experiences and must now be considered.

Chapter Four

COLOUR

COLOUR describes those sensations produced in the brain as rays of differing wavelength impinge upon the eye's retina. Light is a form of electromagnetic radiation and all the wavelengths to which the eye is sensitive lie between approx. 380–760 mμ. Yet though the eye is sensitive to such a narrow waveband it is said that, depending upon the light and the viewer's visual ability, up to ten million different colours can be detected. The rich variety of colour even in comparatively drab surroundings may not always be realised. Colour plays an important, though often unrecognised part in product design. It may be used to help ease product operation, to make the product acceptable in its intended environment or to identify the product manufacturer. In practice these aims are usually interlinked but in the majority of cases, and certainly with engineering equipment, an ergonomic approach to the use of colour should take precedence.

At base colour detection depends upon three factors, namely:

1. The nature of the light falling upon the object being viewed.
2. The nature of the object.
3. The viewer's visual characteristics.

Therefore in order to make a study of colour each of these factors will be briefly studied before defining colour terms and discussing the influence of colour combinations. The use of colour on engineering equipment can then be considered in more detail.

4.1 COLOUR AND LIGHT

White light or daylight contains all the wavelengths in the visible spectrum. This range of wavelengths is shown in Table 4.1.

But while white light is composed of all the frequencies, it can be produced by an appropriate mixture of red, green and blue light. These colours are usually called the primary light colours. By varying the amounts of red, green and blue light in any mixture, all other colours in the spectrum can be composed. A mixture of red and green light produces yellow, while red and blue light produces purple. Since red mixed with green light produces yellow, a mixture of yellow and blue light can, in appropriate quantities, produce white light.

The nature of the light falling upon an object can have a marked influence upon the object's colour. Changes in the colour of objects viewed under daylight, fluorescent and tungsten lighting are well known, though the observer may well recognise a colour as it appears under daylight condition even when the character of the light is markedly different from daylight. This latter aspect, usually called 'colour constancy', will be mentioned again.

However, extreme changes of light can make colour detection difficult. One of the most dramatic changes occurs between viewing

Table 4.1. THE RANGE OF WAVELENGTHS
FOR THE SEVEN PRINCIPAL COLOURS THAT
GO TO MAKE UP THE SPECTRUM OF WHITE
LIGHT

Colour	Wavelength (mμ)
Violet	380–420
Indigo	420–450
Blue	450–490
Green	490–560
Yellow	560–590
Orange	590–630
Red	630–760

an object under daylight conditions and then under the sodium lighting used to illuminate some roads and streets. The sodium light is so restricted in the yellow part of the spectrum that colour discrimination is practically eliminated. Therefore when deciding upon the colour for any piece of equipment it is always necessary to know the type of light under which it will be viewed.

4.2 COLOUR AND OBJECTS

When light falls upon an object, some wavelengths will be absorbed and some reflected, depending upon the nature or pigmentation of the object's surface. The reflected wavelengths determine the object's colour. Thus when viewed under daylight, an object looks red when its surface pigment subtracts all wavelengths except the 'red wavelengths' which it reflects. This leads to a set of primary colours for pigments which is different from the primary light colours. The primary pigment colours, with which the artist or designer is more familiar, are red, blue and *yellow*. These pigment colours can be united to produce all other pigment colours, except white. For example blue mixed with yellow produces green, while red and blue produce purple. But if red, blue and yellow pigments are mixed together in appropriate quantities the result, in theory though seldom in practice, will be black. Because the colour of a pigment is decided by the wavelengths it subtracts from the incident light, a primary pigment is sometimes described as a subtractive primary. This distinguishes it from a light primary, which may be referred to as an additive primary, since when coloured light is mixed, the lights of different wavelengths are being blended together.

Bearing in mind the subtractive nature of pigments, the effects of different types of light falling upon an object can be assessed. For example a surface which is red under daylight conditions will tend towards black when viewed under green light since the pigment absorbs green. Where lighting tends towards the red end of the spectrum then reddish pigments will appear more roseate and yellow may seem brighter while other colours may tend to appear greyer. The opposite effect occurs when lighting tends towards the blue end of the spectrum.

The surface finish of an object can influence its characteristic colour. If the object has a glossy surface it will, depending upon its shape and the directional qualities of the incident light, produce highlights which may overpower the object's characteristic colour. All the light may be reflected and perhaps cause glare which can impede a machine operator's vision as discussed earlier. But those areas where highlights do not occur may appear richer in colour than if they had a matt finish.

Colour can have a strong influence upon the apparent form of an object. In general, light colours will tend to make an object seem

PLATE 5.2 'Purpose' is enhanced by giving the beam of this mixing machine a beam-like appearance even though the top and bottom surfaces are in fact parallel. Maker: Kenwood. Consultant industrial designer: K. Grange (Photograph by courtesy of Kenwood Manufacturing Ltd. & C.o.I.D.)

(a) Baker microscope
(Courtesy: Vickers Ltd.)

PLATES 5.3(a) & (b) 'Purpose' enhanced by more clearly defining structural features. The limb of the microscope in (b) looks more like a column and beam structure which functionally is the case: yet this microscope is different from conventional types of microscope. Maker: Vickers. Consultant industrial designers: London and Upjohn

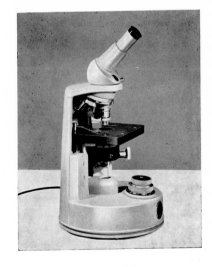

(b) Vickers microscope
(Courtesy: Vickers Ltd.)

(a)

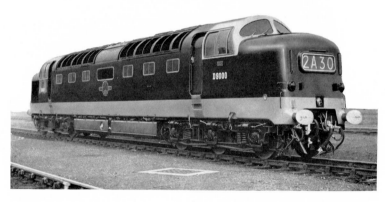

(b)

PLATE 5.4(a) & (b) *The locomotive in (b) looks more powerful and efficient than in (a) largely due to the better panel treatment and removal of superfluities—decorative devices in particular! But this is no proof that it is in fact a better machine. Maker: English Electric. Consultant industrial designers: J. Howe for British Rail Design Panel (Photographs by courtesy of British Rail)*

PLATES 6.1 *A good house style emerges from careful attention to everything produced by a company as shown by the products, exhibition equipment and publicity material produced by I.B.M.*

(a) *Above: I.B.M. Tape unit (Photograph Rome Studio Ltd.)*
(b) *Below: I.B.M. Stand at Olympia*
    (Photograph: D. C. Morris & Co., London, S.W.9.)

PLATES 6.1 (*Continued:*)
(c) *Above: Examples of I.B.M. catalogues*
(*Photograph: C.o.I.D.*)
(d) *Below: I.B.M. 72 Electric typewriter*
(*Photograph: C.o.I.D.*)

light in weight while dark colours may make it seem heavy. These tendencies can be used to good effect in machine design and will be referred to again. Clearly different colours reflect different amounts of light. The level of illumination in a room with dark grey walls is obviously less than if the walls were white, though lit by the same light source. Table 4.2 gives a rough indication of the percentage of incident light reflected from a variety of surface colours.

Table 4.2. THE REFLECTING POWER OF DIFFER-
ENT COLOURED SURFACES OF EQUIVALENT SUR-
FACE FINISH

Colour of the Surface	Percentage of Incident Light Reflected
White	85
Light grey	76
Light yellow	75
Light green	65
Light blue	55
Medium grey	65
Medium yellow	52
Medium green	35
Medium blue	30
Dark grey	30
Dark red	13
Dark green	7
Dark blue	8

Though approximate, these reflection values provide a sufficiently adequate guide for most purposes.

4.3 COLOUR AND THE EYE

As noted earlier, the eye's retina has two types of receptor, namely rods and cones; the approximate distribution of these receptors being shown in Fig. 3.2 (a), Section 3.1. Rods can only perceive black, white and shades of grey. On the other hand cones enable colour perception at least as long as the illumination is above a certain level which is about 0·001 lm/ft². Below this level of illumination no colour can be detected. Between 0·0100 and 0·001 lm/ft² the eyes have so-called twilight vision. As illumination decreases in this twilight range, red and yellow colours grow dimmer and finally become shades of grey.

E

Meanwhile green and blue hold their colour until lower levels of illumination are reached. But on reaching 0·001 lm/ft² these too become shades of grey.

When the cone system is fully operative, colour detection is thought to occur by the manner in which the cones are interlinked and connected to the brain by way of the optic nerve. An earlier theory suggested that there are three types of cone, each responsive to a different light primary. Thus by supposing that one set of cones responds to red, another to blue and another to green, it was inferred that a colour 'picture' is built up in much the same way as in colour printing or photography. However examination of cones has not shown any difference in their character to support this theory. It seems that the somewhat complex system of interconnections between the cones and the brain is the more likely means by which colour detection is possible. Nevertheless the concept of building up a picture from the primary light colours, red, blue and green, can be used to describe two important aspects of colour in relation to the eye. These are after-image and colour-blindness.

4.3.1 AFTER-IMAGE

After-images may occur after the eye has been forced to concentrate upon an object whose colour contrasts strongly with its background. If a red spot on a white ground is stared at for about two minutes, the eye on moving to view a clear white ground will see a greenish-blue image of the spot. A simple explanation of this effect is that the nerve system signalling 'red' to the brain has become tired so that when looking at white the eye sees white *minus* red to produce the greenish-blue effect.

This type of after-image is known as a negative after-image. It can occur with black and white, as may be noted by staring at the figure and ground illustrations in Fig. 3.6, Section 3.2. A really concentrated stare at these illustrations will produce reversals; black becoming white in the after-image. However if these illustrations are stared at for only a short time, positive after-images may be seen; that is the after-images will correspond with the illustrations. The possible explanation for positive after-images is that the nerve system is retaining its stimulus and has not reached the tired state which produces negative images.

The persistence of after-images depends very much upon the intensity of the illumination, the amount of contrast between figure and ground and the time over which the figure is steadily examined. It is possible that after-images are being constantly seen but seldom realised since they may be absorbed into the prevailing background. One advantage of painting hospital operating theatres green is that this colour absorbs the green after-images which may follow a surgeon's protracted concentration upon blood-coloured areas. There are a number of manufacturing circumstances where a similar degree of concentration may be involved, consequently selection of colours which will absorb negative after-images becomes important.

4.3.2 COLOUR-BLINDNESS

Although it has been said that the eye can differentiate up to ten million colours, recognition may be restricted by various forms of colour-blindness. Strictly speaking colour-blindness implies a total lack of colour recognition. A completely colour-blind person would see only black, white and shades of grey. But while very few people suffer total colour-blindness, up to 8% of the male population has one or other type of deficiency in colour recognition. Colour-blindness is generally hereditary though it can occur through illness. However, it is seldom found in women. Normal colour vision can be said to occur if the three light primaries are being received. A weak form of colour deficiency occurs with those who, though responsive to the light primaries, need them in excessive amounts. Such people may be hard to identify without using refined tests. More easily detected are those who either cannot recognise red—the red-blind, or those unable to recognise green—the green-blind. Thus the spectrum of colours which each type can observe, is made up from two colours rather than the three colours available to those with normal colour vision. For red-blind or green-blind people, only blue and yellow remain unconfused. The incidence of colour-blindness may make it necessary to support warning or coding systems based on specified colours with words or symbols. However many people may have one or other type of colour-blindness and never, unless tested, appreciate their deficiency. They 'cue' their responses according to those of others and by long-standing experience.

4.4 COLOUR CONSTANCY

It was noted earlier that the colour of an object will change according
to the light under which it is viewed. However this change may not
always be recognised. By long association with the characteristic
colours of natural features, thus white is the characteristic colour of
snow, an observer will still call snow white though it may be seen
under twilight conditions. Colour constancy is clearly a mental rather
than an optical aspect of colour recognition.

But before considering in more detail the general influence of
colours and colour combinations on the mind, it is necessary to define
the terms used to identify different colours.

4.5 COLOUR TERMS

The descriptions 'light-grey' or 'dark-red' are obviously inadequate as
colour specifications—consequently colour terms in general use and
the systems used to specify any particular colour should be understood.
To begin with, it is useful to identify two main types of colour:

1. *Chromatic colour*, that is any colour which lies within the spectrum
   red to violet, and
2. *Achromatic colour*, that is white through all shades of grey to
   black.

A system for colour identification was established in 1931 by the
Commission Internationale de l'Eclairage and is generally known as the
C.I.E. system. It is based upon defining a colour by comparing it with
a measured mixture of the three light primaries which would produce
the equivalent colour. The system is comparatively technical and is
used mainly for accurate colour matching. It need not be considered
further except to say that one of the several systems of colour identification, the Munsell system, is linked with it. These systems are all
based on the colour circle.

4.5.1 THE COLOUR CIRCLE

This is a form of colour chart first devised by Sir Isaac Newton. Newton
arranged the colours of the spectrum as in Fig. 4.1. However others,
notably Ives, Ostwald and Munsell have also produced colour circles.

Newton based his circle on 7 colours, while as shown on Fig. 4.1, Ives used 3 colours, Ostwald 4, and Munsell 5. All these circles have two things in common. First, diagonally opposing colours are referred to as opposite complementary colours. Thus in the Munsell system, blue-green and red are opposite complementaries. It will be remembered that the negative after-image of red is blue-green, so that, at

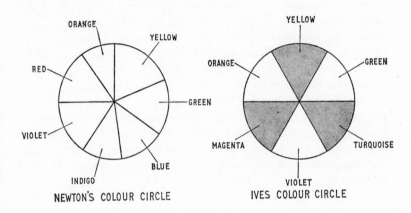

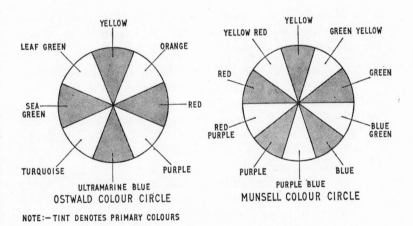

NOTE:— TINT DENOTES PRIMARY COLOURS

FIG. 4.1 *Colour circles for classifying colours. The Munsell system is now the most commonly used*

least with the Munsell system, an assessment of after-image can be obtained by identifying the opposite complementary of any colour likely to be studied for protracted periods. Secondly, all of these circles can be expanded at will by mixing adjacent colours. Suppose for example, that a colour circle has three basic colours red, blue and yellow. It can be expanded to six colours to give red, purple, blue, green, yellow and orange. This colour circle is probably familiar to all those who have taken elementary art lessons. Purple, green and orange are obtained by mixing red and blue, blue and yellow, and yellow and red respectively. They are sometimes called secondary colours to distinguish them from the basic and so-called primary colours.

The difference between Ives, Ostwald and Munsell colour circles is simply the difference in the quality of the colours chosen as basic colours. While the Ives and Ostwald systems are in use, the Munsell system may be favoured particularly in determining pigments for industrial equipment. This is because it is related to the C.I.E. system of measurement. Colour specifications produced by the British Standards Institution are based upon the Munsell system of colour notation.

4.5.2 MUNSELL COLOUR NOTATION

In the Munsell system a colour is described in terms of *Hue*, *Chroma* and *Value*. These are arranged in ordinate form as shown in Fig. 4.2. They are interpreted as follows:

1. *Hue* distinguishes one chromatic colour from another. Hues form the colour circle located about the vertical axis in Fig. 4.2 and conform with the Munsell system of distribution in Fig. 4.1.
2. *Chroma* describes the purity of a colour in respect of the amount of grey which may be present in it. A colour of strong chroma will have little grey, while a colour with weak chroma will approach neutral grey.
3. *Value* describes the lightness or darkness of a colour. The lighter the colour the higher its value. A light green therefore has a high value while a dark green has a low value.

The Munsell system arbitrarily divides hue, value and chroma into regular stepped changes and the variations are charted in a forty-page

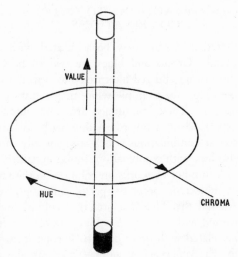

FIG. 4.2 *Munsell colour ordinates. Hue distinguishes one chromatic colour from another, value describes its lightness or darkness and chroma defines its purity. At the central axis 'colour' moves from black to white, being mid-grey in the plane of the hue circle*

atlas. This atlas forms the basis for colour selection and specification. For example, *BS:2660, Colours for Building and Decorative Paints*, produced by the British Standards Institution, gives 103 colours selected from the Munsell atlas.

4.5.3 OTHER COLOUR TERMS

Perhaps one difficulty with the Munsell system is that the expressions hue, value and chroma may not be as familiar as others. A number of expressions are frequently used rather loosely and without regard for their real meaning. This is particularly the case with expressions tone, tint and shade which are often used as supposed alternatives to the word colour itself. But to be precise, *Tone* is equivalent to *value*. The tonal range of say red extends from pale red approaching white to deep red approaching black. *Tint* should be reserved for any colour of high value, while *Shade* should be used for any colour of low value. Light red is a tint while dark red is a shade.

Currently, the word tone may be used more frequently than value, while saturation may be used more frequently than chroma. On occasions the expressions intensity and purity may also be used instead of chroma or saturation.

4.6 REACTIONS TO COLOUR AND COLOUR COMBINATIONS

Different colours may be associated with or even inspire different moods. Greens and blues are said to be cool, yellow regarded as stimulating and red interpreted as warm. Colours may also be given meanings, for example white may signify purity or red may suggest danger. These meanings are undoubtedly acquired from past experience or from association with colours in nature. In addition, colour combinations which are generally thought to be pleasing may also link with combinations found in nature.

A number of works on colour give the results of tests on a variety of subjects in order to specify colour preferences. For example it is asserted that blue is a preferred colour. Such preferences should be treated with caution. A colour is never seen in isolation. It is bound to be related with other colours. Further it may have a special meaning for the observer. A woman may say she dislikes yellow, possibly because she feels that yellow clothing would not suit her facial or hair colouring. A man might express an aversion for pink, but only because he may regard it as a 'feminine' colour and thus not one which he would choose for his own attire. Yet both man and woman would quite happily accept these colours in what they regard as their proper place.

When colours are combined in a colour scheme, they may appear to change in character from when they are seen singly. A colour on a dark ground will look lighter or, using the appropriate colour terms, have a higher value, than when seen on a light ground. In addition two other apparent changes can be noted. A hue composed of two adjacent basic hues in a colour circle and standing on a ground composed of one of these hues, will tend to lose the quality possessed by its ground. For example orange standing on a yellow ground will look more red, while if placed on a red ground it will look more yellow. Turquoise, or blue-green will look more green on a blue ground and more blue on a green ground. Finally a colour's chroma or purity may appear to alter according to the amount of grey in the ground. It will look purer or more saturated on a grey ground and less pure when seen on a highly saturated ground.

These effects must be taken into account when deciding upon a colour scheme for any product. Ideally colours should be compared either by putting together samples in the combination they will form on the product or by experiment on a model. Where a small model or small samples are used it should be noted that the colours will generally look stronger or purer than they will when applied to the full sized unit. Hues which may seem too brilliant on a small model may become more acceptable when seen in their true scale. Nevertheless a model can aid assessment of apparent changes when different colours are related to one another.

4.6.1 HARMONIES

Relationships which have a pleasing effect are loosely described as harmonies. Different types of colour harmony have been propounded by colour theorists but these should not be regarded as the only harmonies which can be created. Colours can be combined in an infinite number of ways. There may be more harmonies than those described here.

It can be safely asserted that any pure hue will go with black or white. Any tint will harmonise with white, while any shade will harmonise with black. It can also be asserted that an observer tends to

(a)   (b)   (c)

FIG. 4.3 *Colour, or, as in this case tonal changes, should be distinct. (a) may seem confused compared with (b), but (c) is also confusing as there is no orderly arrangement*

appreciate an orderly sequence of colour and wants to see each colour as fairly distinct from its neighbours. Fig. 4.3 shows variations of grey where in (a) the differences are indistinct and so create a confusing impression by comparison with (b). Fig. 4.3 (c) shows a lack of sequence which in general may not be found so acceptable as (b).

Sequential harmonies may be produced with hues by moving round the colour circle in discrete steps. Thus a simple harmony will be achieved with yellow, yellow-orange and orange. Another sequential harmony might be green, yellow-green and yellow. Harmonies of this kind can be linked with the moods and feelings which some colours seem to generate. A sequence from blue to green will have a cool effect, while yellow to red will produce a warm effect.

Harmonies can be obtained by using opposite complimentary colours such as red and blue-green. Contrast harmonies of this kind create more attention but have to be treated with caution. A contrast formed from approximately equal amounts of opposite complimentary colour may well produce a dazzling effect, especially if the colours are of equal value. Red lettering on a blue-green ground might seem to create attention since the greatest colour contrast is being used. However if the area of lettering is roughly equal to the ground, the lettering will be difficult to read. In general, contrast harmonies are best when one colour is featured on a ground of larger area. If more variety is required two colours which are in sequence on the colour circle may be matched with the opposite complimentary of a mixture of these two colours. Again equal distribution of colour may be less effective than the use of two colours in smaller amounts compared with the ground upon which they stand. More complex harmonies may be produced by combining three or four hues selected from equally spaced positions around the colour circle. However, these are more likely to interest the artist or graphic designer than the designer of engineering equipment.

In addition to harmonies achieved by selecting hues from the colour circle, harmonies may also be obtained by combining tints with shades or by selecting a range of so-called neutral colours such as greys and browns. Further, hues can be combined with neutral colours, say yellow with a range of browns to give a warm effect or blue with a range of greys to give a cool effect. When such combinations are used it is usually better to avoid pure hues and to choose hues with a trace of the colours with which they are matched. When combining tints with shades, tints of colours which reflect most light such as orange, yellow and green, will generally relate better with shades of those colours having lower reflectance such as blue and purple. A combination of light yellow and deep blue will usually be preferred to deep yellow with light blue.

It must be stressed that the foregoing outlines should not be interpreted too literally. But they may provide a basis for practical experiment which could lead to the discovery of other harmonies. In making such experiments in relation to products, choice of colour combinations must be related with the purpose and form of the product and the environment for which it is intended.

4.7 COLOUR ON ENGINEERING EQUIPMENT

Colour selection on engineering equipment should begin with its use in an ergonomic context. The first point to appreciate is that the product is a light absorber. If it is painted in a dark colour, say the familiar battleship-grey, then, if very large, it will cut down the general level of illumination when installed in a factory. In general, factory installed equipment is better painted in light colours. However colours which are too light may encourage glare. Further in some circumstances, it may be almost impossible to keep very light surfaces clean. High gloss surfaces, though generally capable of withstanding wear more readily than matt surfaces, may also create glare especially where lighting is of a directional nature.

Non-reflecting finishes which have good wear resistance are especially useful in the control and work regions of machinery. A change of colour between the structure of the machine and control or work areas, helps in obtaining ready identification of these areas and the operating features within them. The small milling machine, Plate 4.1 is an excellent example of this approach. The control panel, in a light colour, tends to have a slightly phototropic effect in drawing the eye to it. Excessive contrasts between structural surrounds and work or control areas should be avoided, whether these areas are made darker or lighter than their surrounds. For example, a light grey control area will provide sufficient contrast with a medium grey surround to enable it to be discerned. It is not necessary to go to such extremes as black and white. Indeed, since the eye is, as it were, constantly in motion when observing any particular area, very sharp contrasts between a control area and its surround can be tiring. Clearly if the surround is extremely slender the question of strong contrast is not so important.

In general, strong contrasts should be reserved for features requiring interpretation such as visual indicators, printed instructions and the like. In most cases these are best in black and white, provided care is taken to ensure that they are not used in equal amounts. As when using equal amounts of opposite complementary colours, equal amounts of black and white may well create dazzle. On complex machinery, colour variations can be used to advantage within the control or work areas. A large control panel may carry several control areas each having a particular function. These areas may be defined by colour variation but care has to be taken that the contrasts are not excessive. Differences of tone may well be adequate; and these differences should usually be less than the difference between the whole panel and its surround. Within work areas, moving elements and guarded equipment can be shown in different colours and possibly given a stronger treatment. However, this does not imply the use of full hues. Comparatively subtle changes of colour can easily be discerned and the use of full hues may be distracting if an operator is required to concentrate on his work. Choice of colours for work areas should be made with the possibility of after-image effects in mind and also so that the work being viewed is clearly seen against its background. Once again strong contrasts are not usually needed. Black or dark grey backgrounds may not be necessary to identify the work in metalworking tools.

4.7.1 COLOUR CODING

The use of colour for coding purposes can be regarded in an ergonomic context. The essential requirement is that the meaning given to the colour should be clearly understood. This may mean that colours chosen for any coding systems should conform with the 'meanings' which are generally given to some colours. Obviously red, denoting 'danger' or 'stop', cannot be easily used for other purposes. Colour code standards are produced by all national standards organisations and these should be studied and used especially where questions of safety are involved. But safety code colours should not be used excessively. For example, orange is used to signify electrical systems in factory installations and is sometimes applied to all electrical equipment as a result. The effect may be extremely distracting. Further the code colour may tend to lose its significance.

A small amount of safety colour, located so that it can be seen and if possible at the points considered to be most dangerous, is more effective than a total treatment.

In highly dangerous situations account must be taken of the incidence of colour blindness when using safety colours. It is always advisable to supplement warning colours with words identifying the danger.

4.7.1.1 *Coding machine internals*

Bearing in mind that the lighter the colour the more light is kept in circulation, machine internals should be in light colours in order to assist assembly and maintenance. The insides of cover panels and inspection doors must be painted in a bright hue in order that they can be seen if they are removed or left ajar. Colour coding of components or sub-assemblies can considerably aid assembly and servicing, particularly in complex installations. Colour coding may also be adopted to identify areas which have to be serviced at different intervals of time or, as in one known case, areas which may be serviced by the user against areas which should only be serviced by the maker.

4.7.1.2 *Coding mobile equipment*

Mobile equipment whether inside or outside the factory, should be clearly discernible against its normal background. Cranes, fork lift trucks, trolleys, trucks and so on must be clearly seen. On this type of equipment full hues become permissible. However they should not be allowed to obtrude excessively on their operators' vision. In order to create maximum attention it may be necessary to use strong contrasts such as the black and yellow banding used on the buffer beams of shunting engines. If this is necessary then bold bands of colour are to be preferred. Full hues may well be useful on such external equipment as pneumatic road drills, compressors and farm machinery.

4.7.2 PSYCHOLOGICAL EFFECTS

Finally, while keeping first to an ergonomic use of colour, general psychological effects should not be overlooked. For example, while hot or warm environments will not in fact be cooler by using 'cool' colours, they can influence those who have to work in them. Rolling mills and heat treatment workshops can be 'cooled' by using grey-greens and blues. On the other hand a cold environment may be 'warmed' by the use of warmer colours. These aspects may be more the concern of the factory designer but they should not be overlooked by the designer whose machinery will occupy a large part of the factory environment.

The machine designer may have to guard against using colours which, although acceptable in his own society, may cause offence or be misinterpreted in another society. Intended markets should be investigated in order to ensure that this does not occur. However, a distinction should be drawn between colours which have come to have a 'social meaning', however illogical it may seem, and colours which are regarded as 'right' for the equipment being used but which could in fact be improved. For example, until recently microscopes were supposed to be black while a great deal of engineering equipment was painted in battleship-grey since this colour was supposed to underline its character. It may be necessary to make cautious changes where colours have come to have longstanding meanings of this kind, even if new colours will enable easier machine operation. Also, in some cases, it may be necessary to consider using different colour ranges depending upon the markets in which the products will be sold.

4.7.3 COLOUR AND MACHINE FORM

Colour has a strong influence upon the apparent form of an object. Dark colours giving the effect of weight may be used on foundations or main supporting structures in order to underline their character, while light colours may be used to minimise the effect of masses which might otherwise create a top-heavy effect. Thus colour can support form in clearly describing a machine's purpose or structural composition. But it can seldom be made to obscure form. Fig. 4.4 (a) shows a machine on which an attempt has been made to outline a beam form at the top. Apart from the practical difficulty of painting one surface in two different colours, the effect is entirely artificial. A preferred colour scheme is shown in Fig. 4.4 (b) where in addition a dark colour has been applied to the base to emphasise its mass.

A lack of harmony in the colours chosen can easily spoil attempts to create a unified appearance in a product. So it may seem that if painted in one colour there will be no danger of this occurring.

However, a single-colour treatment, particularly if the colour verges on a full hue, may well destroy a machine's character. The locomotive in Plate 4.2 (*a*), painted to customer's requirements, shows a loss of character by comparison with the consultant designer's scheme in Plate 4.2 (*b*). Here colour has been used to support a sense of structural order and so subscribe to an overall impression of unity.

Despite the different ways in which colour can be applied to ergonomic advantage, the number of colours used should be kept to a minimum. While this may be necessary on the practical grounds of cost, it also helps to avoid too much variety. In many cases a two-colour or three-colour treatment can produce all that is needed. Variations need not be made by changing hue. Changes of tone, say a

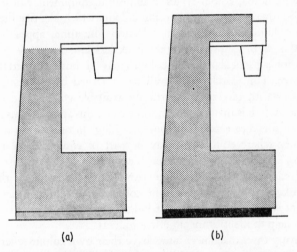

(a)   (b)

Fig. 4.4 *Attempts to create effects by ignoring structural composition usually fail. In (a) the top of the machine is made to look like a beam but the structure does not support this impression. The paint scheme shown in (b) is preferable*

range of greys or greens may well be sufficient, particularly if hues are used for control knobs, pushbuttons and the like or for safety systems.

Economy in the use of colour on machinery helps in relating it to its intended environment. Too many colours are likely to make a machine unnecessarily conspicuous and may well tend to lower its apparent worth by making it appear garish.

4.7.4 COLOUR AND STYLE

Engineering based consumer products are strongly influenced by trends in the colours chosen for interior decoration and even clothing. But since they are of a more transitory nature, these trends should not unduly influence selection of colours for general industrial equipment. Such changes may well follow social changes. For example, after the Second World War people were attracted by bright colours as a reaction to four drab war years. Subsequently pastel shades emerged to be replaced later by mixtures of browns and tans, these latter colours usually forming backgrounds for richer combinations of hue. Bearing this in mind, colour selection for consumer products can become the task of a specialist with means for analysing market tendencies.

But while changes in colour styles in other design fields should always be noted, colour styles in industrial equipment will generally depend rather more upon choosing colours which identify the manufacturer. Unfortunately colour selection sometimes appears to start with this as the most important consideration. In many cases, the search for a particular 'house colour' may be both exasperating and expensive. This search could well be shortened by adopting a two-colour system, relying upon readily available colours and ensuring that this system is maintained. In some cases, this approach may relieve the need for very accurate colour matching. In other cases however, especially where equipment may be part of composite or modular systems, accurate colour matching is essential. Checks may have to be made that colours avoid metamerism. Briefly this means that two pigments, apparently identical in colour in one light, may appear different when seen in a different light. Investigations using the C.I.E. system help to identify metameric pigments.

In many cases machinery users have their own colour schemes and the maker supplies his machinery accordingly. But bearing in mind that equipment is displayed either in exhibitions or in advertisements, a 'house colour' system can help to establish a maker's identity. Surface finish should not be overlooked in this context, for surface finish is a salient pointer to the care with which the product has been constructed. It is unnecessary to embellish machinery with chromium plating to create an impression of fine workmanship. This is sometimes attempted together with the use of high gloss finishes. The result is usually a lowering rather than an increase in apparent worth while creating

COLOUR 81

unnecessary visual distraction for the machine operator. First and foremost, colour should be regarded as a tool to help the operator then
as a means for supporting the aesthetic objectives outlined in Chapter
Five before becoming concerned with style. It is important to stress
this point. All too frequently colours are chosen by personal whim
and without regard for its value in the ergonomic sense. The
emotional influences of colour so often seem to override attempts at
making a more thoughtful approach to its application. But this more
intellectual approach is essential when designing industrial equipment.
It will not lead to defining particular colours but it will determine
ranges of colour from which particular colours can be chosen.

F

Chapter Five

AESTHETIC CONCEPTS

A DICTIONARY definition of aesthetics is that it is concerned with the study or appreciation of beauty. This definition may tend to create a number of impressions which, on reflection, cannot be upheld. For example, it might suggest that beauty is something real and external to an observer. In using the word 'study' the definition might also suggest that beauty can be analysed. Then if it can be analysed it might also be measured. These last two thoughts could well appeal to the engineer who is used to processes of analysis and measurement. But common experience shows that beauty is in the eye of the beholder. People often disagree over what is or is not thought to be beautiful. Even when they do agree, the intensity of their appreciation may be different. An aesthetic experience can be so strong as to evoke an intense emotional surge or it may be merely a mild awareness of something pleasing.

Because the appreciation of beauty is a highly personal experience, it might seem to form a subject for psychological study. In fact, studies of this kind have been undertaken. In the main they have been conducted by asking groups of people to show their preferences when faced with various comparatively simple shapes. Such tests produce at least three difficulties. First, simple abstract shapes seen in isolation are by no means equivalent to the complexity of forms and colours which make up our normal environment. Second, it may be questioned whether a majority preference for a particular shape can be taken as indicating beauty. Finally, it may also be questioned whether reactions even to simple shapes are concerned solely with appreciating beauty. For example a shape could conceivably have a particular meaning for one observer and not for another. This meaning might be related with some highly personal experience which could bias the observer's reaction.

Despite these difficulties, further study might lead to more understanding of a subject which has intrigued and tantalised artists and philosophers for centuries. It may be felt that to investigate aesthetic responses by scientific means is to destroy them; rather as if knowledge of how a rainbow is formed might imply that it will no longer be regarded as beautiful. But if psychological tests help to produce information which can be used to enhance human environments then clearly they are worth undertaking. At least such tests might confirm some of the concepts which have been propounded by various students of aesthetics.

In considering these concepts it must be realised that they are not rules or formulae to be applied to product design in the same way as an engineer would use a mathematical equation. Further and most important, a product cannot be studied to see if it embodies any of these concepts and then, if thought to do so, be pronounced aesthetically satisfying. An aesthetic response may not always be immediate but it cannot be contrived. However, when an object or product appeals to the observer, he may well find in subsequent study that the appeal rests on one or, as is more likely, a combination of these concepts.

5.1 THE CONCEPT OF UNITY

The concept of unity appears frequently though in various guises in studies of aesthetics. During the Italian Renaissance a number of attempts were made to formulate 'principles of beauty'. In one attempt, Alberti underlines the concept of beauty in the following words—'I shall define beauty to be a harmony of all the parts in whatsoever subject it appears, fitted together with such proportions and connections that nothing could be added, diminished or altered but for the worse'. It is clear that Alberti's statement is not a formula. The expression 'but for the worse' gives the game away, for different people may have different ideas of what is worse or better if anything were 'added, diminished or altered'. Indeed Alberti's statement may

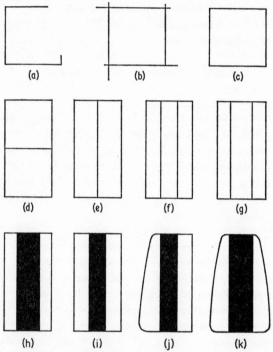

FIG. 5.1 *The concept of unity illustrated in diagrammatic fashion. See text*

seem little more than a tortuous way of saying that something is enjoyed because of the way it all fits together.

However, this simpler interpretation overlooks three main aspects of unity which can be extracted from Alberti's statement. First, the subject should appear to be complete; no part should appear to be missing nor should there appear to be any superfluous elements. Second, there should be a harmonious relationship between all the parts contributing to the whole. And third, emphasis is placed on actually seeing the subject as a whole and not regarding any one part of it to the exclusion of others.

These points may be underlined by the semi-diagrammatic illustrations in Fig. 5.1. The first trio tend to make the first point. (*a*) is clearly incomplete, while in (*b*) the extensions are superfluous. In general (*c*) would be preferred to (*a*) and (*b*). The second point may be illustrated by the next pair, (d) and (e). Taking rectangle (d) to have one side twice as long as the other, a division across the long side produces two squares. The square is such a dominant shape that in (d) the eye tends to see two squares, one on top of the other, rather than the whole rectangle. This effect is sometimes called 'duality'. Duality in appearance can occur, not only when the subject appears to be composed of two visually dominant elements with similar character-istics, but also with dominant elements of dissimilar character. If the rectangle is divided down its length, as in (e), its overall quality is retained since the two long rectangles produced by the central line have a less dominant character.

Arranging component parts to produce an apparent whole may be a highly sensitive process. As shown by (f), it may not be simply a matter of making them identical. Here, there is a tendency to see three equal strips joined together rather than the rectangle as a whole. But when the central strip is increased in width, as in (g) an impression of unity returns, possibly because the centre-piece seems to be buttressed by those on either side of it. This configuration can be found in a variety of subjects; perhaps the most popular being statuary where a central and dominant figure is flanked by lesser figures. Illustrations (h) and (i) underline the sensitivity of judgement which may be needed to make the parts in any subject contribute to the whole. If, as in (h), the central strip is painted black, it may become too dominant and need refining as in (i).

Finally (j) and (k) illustrate the third point extracted from Alberti's statement. Suppose that (j) illustrates the elevation view of a simple container and that its designer has embodied a curved form because he believes this form to be attractive. While it might have appeal when viewed on its own, clearly it looks out of place in the whole assembly. If curvatures are sought, then an arrangement as in (k) might be preferred. Here unity is achieved by balancing the curved form and, at the same time, increasing the width of the central strip because curved lines usually create more attention. Illustration (j) shows the pointlessness of including features which are thought to have intrinsic beauty in order to make the whole attractive. Yet many engineering products can be found which have individual parts fashioned to make them attractive but which in combination fail to subscribe to the concept of unity. These products may have developed in this way because their designers have found they have more freedom with some parts than with others. They have enjoyed themselves fashioning details and have neglected to consider the whole. The approach to unity depends upon constantly keeping the whole subject in mind in order to obtain a successful relationship of its component parts.

5.2 THE CONCEPT OF ORDER WITH VARIETY

If to achieve unity the component elements in a subject should be related to the whole, it may be argued that they should be related to each other. This relationship is usually referred to as order. Thus in music, order is provided by a particular rhythm. However, on its own this rhythm could be extremely monotonous. The music appeals because variations, perhaps a melody, are related with the rhythm. But if such variations were played without any controlling rhythm the listener would probably feel confused. This need for order to be coupled with variety runs through a variety of aesthetic experiences, whether in music, poetry or painting. Roger Fry says in his *Essay in Aesthetics*, 'and the first quality that we demand in our sensations will be order, without which our sensations will be troubled and perplexed, and the other quality will be variety without which they will not be fully stimulated'.

The concept of order with variety stretches through history. Plato called the right-angled triangle which forms half an equilateral triangle the most beautiful since it can be used to build up a variety of shapes, as in Fig. 5.2. As a matter of interest, though certainly not of application, George D. Birkhoff, a mathematician in the U.S.A., tried to produce a formula based upon order and variety. The formula is as follows:

$$M = \frac{O}{C}$$

Where: M = aesthetic measure
i.e. degree of appreciation
O = order
C = complexity or variety

Clearly this formula depends upon the values ascribed to O and C. They must have some limiting values for as C approaches O, M approaches infinity! Professor Eysenck comments more fully on this formula in his book *Sense and Nonsense in Psychology*. He then suggests that the formula M = OC might be more appropriate. However it is unlikely that any formula could be devised to cover the need for order with variety. This may be because it can be interpreted in a number of ways. The terms symmetry, balance, contrast, continuity and proportion can each be regarded in the light of this concept.

As in the section on unity, the semi-diagrammatic illustrations (a)-(e) in Fig. 5.2 may help in picturing this concept. The square (b) has

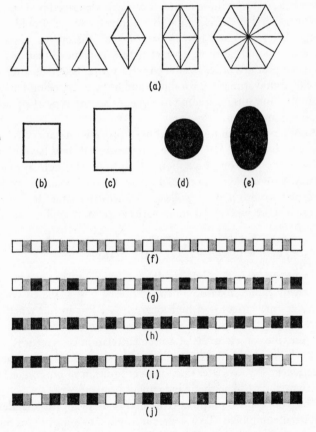

FIG. 5.2 *The concept of order illustrated in diagrammatic fashion. See text*

order but no variety since all sides are equal. Rectangle (c) may be preferred to (b) because, while the shape is still highly ordered, some variety exists in the lengths of the sides. A similar and equally elementary comparison may be made between the circle (d) and the ellipse (e). The circle has no variety; its curvature is constant. But the ellipse though still an orderly shape has a continuously changing curvature.

On occasions some mathematicians like to contend that mathematics is the seat of beauty and that a mathematically generated form is bound to be appreciated. Unfortunately this is not always the case. The circle and the ellipse can each be easily described by mathematics. But in general the circle, though a dominant shape, would hardly be admired, certainly not by comparison with the ellipse. These mathematicians would be more correct if they contended that many equations can produce order combined with variety and that some of these may be found attractive; parabolae and hyperbolae being fairly simple examples. But it is misleading to suggest that any type of equation will inspire appreciation.

Another approach to the concept of order with variety is shown in Fig. 5.2, diagrams (f)-(j). Here progressive changes have been made from a monotonous repetition of squares, through an increasing variety to complete disorder. It may be interesting to pick out a preferred pattern and ask colleagues to do the same. It is sometimes said that those who prefer more variety are more sophisticated!

5.3 THE CONCEPT OF PURPOSE

Later in his *Essay in Aesthetics*, Roger Fry says—'it may be objected that many things in nature, such as flowers, possess these two qualities of order and variety in a high degree. . . . But in our reactions to a work of art there is something more—there is the consciousness of purpose, the consciousness of a peculiar relation of sympathy with the man who made this thing in order to arouse precisely the sensations we experience'. Fry says later that, 'this recognition of purpose is I believe an essential part of aesthetic judgement proper'.

The concept of purpose is especially relevant to the design of industrial equipment. To a degree it implies, to adopt Louis Sullivan's famous dictum, that form should follow function; in other words that what is seen should be descriptive of what is actually there. But as expressed by Fry it suggests something more; a recognition of a personal expression on the part of the designer as if the viewer sees through the created work to the man who made it. It might be supposed that industrial equipment is bound to appear to express its own character whether designers concern themselves with aesthetics or not. However equipment may be found which, possibly due to the successive addition of components and fitments, does not in visual terms tell the observer what it is. F. C. Ashford has pointed out that the appearance of a product is as much a personal statement as if the designer had described it in words. If he had to write a description of his machine, the designer would certainly aim to do so as clearly as possible. And clarity emerges from simplicity. Salient features would be boldly described, minor features played down and those which did not contribute directly to the product's function would be eliminated. The change made in the centre-lathe shown in Plate 5.1 is a good example of producing a clear statement of purpose. Whereas in the earlier machine a variety of elements literally confused the picture, the redesigned version plainly shows the lathe's basic features; a base separated from the work and control area by a horizontal panel (which hides the removable chip tray) and in the working region, plain statements of headstock, bed, carriage and tailstock.

The most successful approach to a clear statement of purpose is made by starting with the simplest sketch of a machine's main elements, almost on a diagrammatic basis. Ideally these elements should bear a character which describes their functions. For example a cantilever beam is normally expected to taper and a block-diagram sketch of such an element might show it in such a form. However in practice, it may be that such an element could not in fact be tapered. The beam of the mixing machine shown in Plate 5.2 is a case in point. Its internal mechanisms require it to be parallel but the designer has held to his beam concept by designing a tapered cover accented by a colour difference and a distinct step between this cover and the underside of the beam casing. This illustration is but one refutation of the belief that 'purpose' is automatically displayed by solving the technical requirements in a design problem. A purely 'technical' solution may succeed in some cases, but it cannot be claimed that it will always succeed. It is worth restating that the external forms of many products cannot be determined entirely by solving technical requirements. In such cases, the designer should start with a simple image which he trys to work towards; establishing main features, playing down minor features and eliminating those which tend to confuse the picture.

In many cases products tend to be judged against those with which the observer is familiar. He establishes 'stereotypes' some of which are so strong that they can hardly be broken. Thus he might be offended if his coffee were poured from a vessel shaped like a teapot. Engineers establish stereotypes in relation to equipment with which they have been familiar for a long time. Indeed the lathe in Plate 5.1 (a) was regarded with some doubt when it first appeared because it was different from other lathes though it is a striking example of showing a lathe in its simplest form. To some extent a clear statement of purpose may be regarded as aiming for a simple stereotype. However, products which have no predecessors are constantly being developed so that the stereotype theory cannot always be applied. All engineers could visualise a lathe and its essential features. But few could determine the characteristics of say a spark-erosion machine, while not many more would recognise one at first sight. What would be recognised and appreciated is the machine's structural composition. If this can be simply expressed, the concept of purpose is being attained though the whole unit may be unfamiliar. The microscope shown in Plate 5.3 helps to make this point. When first built, its manufacturer met some resistance from those who had established stereotypes in relation to the more familiar type of microscope. Owing to the excellent reasons for building a microscope in this manner, this resistance was soon broken down. The microscope, Plate 5.3 (a), was then developed further and in doing so the limb improved to display its function more clearly. Essentially a column and beam, it is shown as such in the improved version Plate 5.3 (b).

5.4 STYLE AND ENVIRONMENT

Unity, order with variety and purpose may be observed in all man's creations, whether they are works of art, buildings, structures or products. In addition, whether produced by artists, architects or engineers, these works will express the personality of their creators. It would be possible for different designers to embody all the foregoing concepts in products performing similar duties yet these products could easily be distinguished from each other. Therefore an aesthetic response may well include recognition of a particular style. Returning to F. C. Ashford's point that a product can be likened to a verbal or literary statement; it may be noted that the merit of a statement depends upon how it is expressed as well as upon what it actually says. On occasions it may be felt that too much attention is paid to 'how', so that the 'subject matter' is overlooked. The result may be a collection of shapes which are thought to give character to the product but which do not support the more fundamental concepts. Yet appreciation of the mode of expression is certainly part of an aesthetic experience.

Architecture and products differ from works of art in that they cannot help but be related with the environment they occupy. Aesthetic appreciation may therefore be conditioned by an observer's reaction not just to the product under view, but to the product as it forms part of his visual scene. Relating the product to its environment could be regarded as another aspect of style and will be considered as such later. However, it has been mentioned here since undoubtedly it plays a part in aesthetic experience.

5.5 AESTHETIC EXPRESSIONS

As mentioned earlier expressions such as *symmetry*, *balance*, *contrast*, *continuity* and *proportion* can be related to the concept of order with variety. These terms are therefore considered in this particular light.

5.5.1 SYMMETRY

Illustrations (*a*), (*b*), (*c*) and (*d*) in Fig. 5.3 have one common quality. Each is symmetrical about one or more axes. Symmetry is familiar to the engineer for many engineering devices must be symmetrical either to achieve their purpose or to enable manufacture. From the aesthetic point of view, symmetry is perhaps the simplest way of achieving order. Possibly for this reason, it is occasionally attempted where either it produces forms which are too orderly or where it serves no useful purpose. Control panels may be found where the control layout does not conform with the way in which the controls

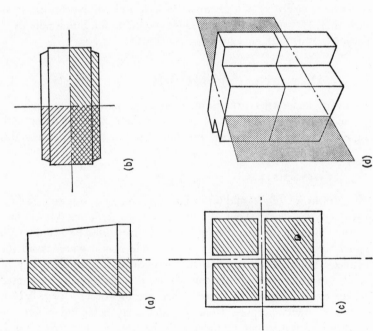

Fig. 5.3 Examples of symmetry, perhaps the easiest way of obtaining an orderly arrangement and for this reason often attempted when unnecessary

(a)

(b)

(c)

(d)

are operated but are set out in some arbitrary symmetrical pattern. Such layouts present a false sense of order and may well be dangerous. Since symmetry frequently develops from the way a product meets technical requirements, little more need be said about it.

5.5.2 BALANCE

Symmetry could be regarded as a balance of two identical features about a point, line or plane. Where the features are not identical and particularly where more than two features are involved, they may need to be arranged so that they appear to balance each other. In other

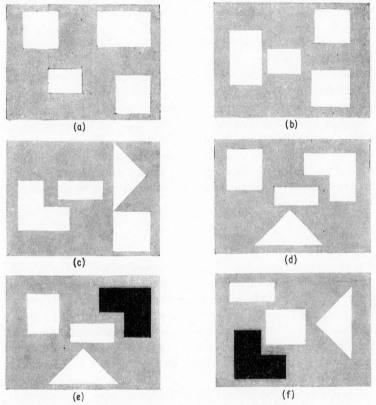

FIG. 5.4 *Simple abstract compositions to illustrate an approach to balancing masses*

words the designer may have to seek a relationship of the parts in order
to make the whole appear unified. Fig. 5.4 puts the subject of balance
into simple visual terms. In (a) the four elements have no apparent
relationship; the whole composition lacks unity. (b) attempts unity
by balancing three elements about a nearly central element. An
engineering analogy might be that the three masses are located by
taking moments of their areas about the central element. However, the
remaining illustrations show that this analogy cannot always be
applied. For example, in (c), locations are approximately identical but
changes in shape have been made. The triangle tends to lead the eye
out of the composition, and a revised composition might be needed
to restore balance and an impression of unity. (d) shows a possible
arrangement with the triangle literally acting as a fulcrum. When the
apparent mass of one element is altered, as in (e), where a dark
colour tends to add weight to the element, a further reordering may
be necessary as in (f).

These examples are, of course, purely illustrative of an approach to
the subject of balance and not to be regarded as having any engineering
meaning. In the design of engineering equipment the salient masses in
a product will almost always be connected together. The approach to
a balanced design will also be made with the concept of purpose very
much in mind. Abstract compositions are extremely useful, both to be
studied and indeed to be attempted in order to assess relationships
between masses; but in engineering design a product is by no means an
abstract composition.

5.5.3 CONTRAST

It is possible to regard contrast as the balance of two elements with
distinctly different characteristics. An analogy with the effects of colour
contrasts can be made here. It may be recalled from Chapter Four that
two contrasting colours juxtaposed in equal amounts may be found
irritating. But if one colour is allowed to act as a background to
the other, then a harmonious relationship will be achieved. Much the
same effect may occur with two dissimilar shapes of approximately
equal apparent mass.

Contrasts create interest and are useful for drawing attention either
to a product or to areas within the product. Possibly for this reason,

extreme contrasts are sometimes attempted and create a confusing or perhaps garish impression. Contrasts can be useful for drawing attention to, say, control or work areas on a machine but they should not be overdone. In general extreme contrasts are not necessary to show up areas to which the eye should be drawn.

5.5.4 CONTINUITY

Continuity could be regarded as simply another word for order. Here it is interpreted as describing any characteristic which may run through a product almost like an underlying rhythm in music. Thus the centre lathe in Plate 5.1 (b) shows continuity in the use of rectangular forms for the main elements. Continuity is also displayed in the identical character of the control levers and handwheels. Continuity may be aided by paying attention to what may seem to be comparatively minor features. The use of equivalent corner radii or similar fixing bolts throughout a product will help visually to tie the whole product together.

Clearly standardisation not only of radii and bolt sizes, but also of such features as bosses on castings, name-plates, visual indicators and control elements can support an impression of continuity through a product.

5.5.5 PROPORTION

Proportion describes the relationship of the main dimensions of a feature or the dimensional relationship of this feature to other features. The beam shaped head of the mixing machine in Plate 5.1 might have been described as out of proportion if it had appeared parallel in form. This judgement might have been made both in terms of the ratio of the beam's length to its depth and also with regard to the apparent size of the beam in relation to the other features. Here, proportion is being judged very much in terms of 'purpose'. Engineers will nearly always judge proportions in such terms and rightly so. However, it is always necessary to guard against too strongly held stereotypes. For example supersonic aircraft with long thin fuselages and short tapered wings seemed 'out of proportion' when they first appeared largely because they were compared with more familiar subsonic types.

The subject of proportion has always been of special interest to the architect and a variety of proportioning systems have been devised to produce an orderly relationship between the component elements of a structure. Referring to Fig. 5.2 the squares in (f) are in the proportion of 1:1 producing, as noted earlier, order with no variety. If each successive square were say doubled in size, then variety is introduced but an underlying order remains. Clearly a host of proportioned relationships could be produced either by geometric or arithmetic series. Of the many systems devised for obtaining an orderly relationship between parts, perhaps the most intriguing one is based upon the *Golden Ratio* or *Phi*.

Phi is an irrational number based upon the ratio shown in Fig. 5.5 (a). This ratio was certainly known to ancient Greek architects and sculptors. Phidias, a famous Greek sculptor, used it in his work, while the Pythagorean brotherhood devised as its symbol a five pointed star based on phi. During the Renaissance, Phi, at that time called the 'divine proportion', seemed to acquire almost mystical properties. It emerged again in the nineteenth century when it received its present name and, once more, a reputation for being almost a formula for beauty. The German psychologist Zeising attempted to show by experiment that people prefer a rectangle which is in Golden Ratio proportion, while Hambidge in the U.S.A. used it in the creation of proportioning systems under the title 'dynamic symmetry'. More recently Le Corbusier applied the Golden Ratio to his famous 'Modulor' proportioning system.

Apart from being intriguing as a mathematical ratio (it is the only number which becomes its own reciprocal by subtracting one), the Golden Ratio can be linked with certain natural growths. Taking the 'golden rectangle' in Fig. 5.5 (b), it can be seen that a square cut from this rectangle leaves a Golden Rectangle. When in turn a square is cut from this rectangle a second Golden Rectangle is produced. This process can be repeated as shown, and by joining successive corners of the golden rectangle a logarithmic spiral is obtained. This spiral may be noted in sea shells. It may also be related to the spacing of leaves on certain plants and to flower petal formations. Here spacings conform with the Fibonacci series of numbers in which every term is the sum of the two preceding terms, thus, 0, 1, 2, 3, 5, 8, 13, 21 .... The ratio of any two consecutive terms comes closer to Phi as the series increases.

Undoubtedly these relationships coupled with its long and somewhat mystical history gave Phi an importance far beyond its worth. There is even now a danger of regarding it as a mathematical means for obtaining good proportions. At base it should serve only to illustrate a way of obtaining order while producing variety. In most engineering

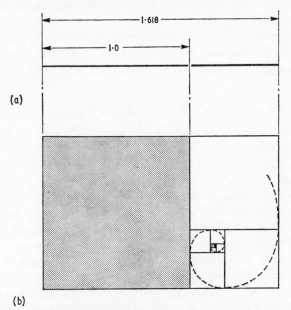

FIG. 5.5 (*a*) *shows the ratio usually known as the Golden Ratio.*
(*b*) *shows a Golden Rectangle where a square cut from the rectangle produces another Golden Rectangle.*
A logarithmic spiral is produced by joining up the corners of successive squares. This spiral is similar to that found in a number of natural features e.g. seashells such as that of the whelk

circumstances there would not be the same degree of freedom to use proportions based on the Golden Ratio, or any other system, as there is in other forms of design work.

Usually it will be found that if a proportioning system is desired (such a system may be useful in obtaining standardised sets of dimensions), then the system will depend upon a careful study of the task in hand. This point is admirably made by Sir Basil Spence though in a quite different field of work. Describing how he tackled the problem

G

of creating unity between the old and new cathedrals at Coventry, he says, 'I found that two separate rhythms existed in the old cathedral, the big rhythm created by the nave pillars and the small one made by the spacing of mullions in the perpendicular tracery. I took these two rhythms and made them into my *blood groups* for the new building. I pursued this course relentlessly; the plan worked out mathematically using these two modules.'

In designing a product, a similar approach, based on maintaining a relationship with its main dimensions, will usually be more rewarding than attempting to adapt any so-called established system.

5.6 A CONCLUSION ON AESTHETICS

It must be restressed that the foregoing aspects of aesthetics should not be taken as rules which, if adhered to, are always bound to produce aesthetic pleasure. Again a product cannot be analysed in terms of these aspects and then judged aesthetically satisfying if it is considered to embody them. Sometimes on examination the concepts studied here may be discerned in what we admire. But sometimes there may be no apparent underlying basis. In the world at large considerable pleasure is gained from natural forms and scenery. Nature can produce orderly forms which are instinctively appreciated but, particularly with natural scenes, the sensations aroused defy any sort of analysis. They can only be interpreted as the artist or writer interprets them by endeavouring to convey his sensations through his chosen medium. In doing so he may well employ a structure upon which he can transmit his feelings. Indeed without such a structure the message he wishes to convey might not be understood. For example, if he is a writer, certain words may spring to mind as apt reflections of his sensations. But a collection of words, however apt in themselves, may have no meaning unless placed in a form which is either familiar to or can be appreciated by the reader. Inevitably the reader's reactions are based upon the words themselves coupled with the structure upon which they have been built. In brief therefore, it is reasonable to take the view that man-made works, as distinct from works of nature, should embody a degree of order and that appreciation will depend upon this order.

In many works of art this order or underlying structure may not be readily discerned. Nor need it be consciously discerned to evoke aesthetic pleasure. But in the design of engineering products it will nearly always be sought. This is because engineering products are the result of applying ordered modes of thinking or scientific principles to achieve a particular task which in itself is usually performed in a highly ordered manner. The two shibboleths 'if it looks right it is right', and 'if it is right it looks right', are based very strongly on this way of thinking. However it is patently obvious that the technical efficiency of a product is no guarantee of aesthetic quality and that the reverse is equally unlikely. The redesigned locomotive in Plate 5.4 (b) looks an improvement on its predecessor largely because ventilators and panelling have been located in a more orderly array. The machine may *look* more efficient but clearly this is no proof that it actually *is* more efficient. The automatic quest for order in the design of engineering products will almost always be accompanied by a desire to see purpose clearly defined. And as pointed out earlier a plain statement of purpose may not necessarily come from only solving the technical requirements.

Thus the perennial question 'what is good design?' (where the word 'design' is used in an aesthetic sense), can only be answered by saying that it will tend to become apparent in engineering products when order and purpose can be discerned. Despite many attempts to phrase more positive answers to this question, this is about as near as one can get to a reply. It must be stressed that this reply is only relevant to engineering products. There are no formulae and no assured ways for creating aesthetic pleasure. But the concepts outlined in this chapter— unity, order with variety and purpose—are worth studying, not only in engineering product design but also in other man-made works. They may often be detected, but not always.

Chapter Six

STYLE

THERE are many products which, while performing identical tasks and possibly giving aesthetic pleasure, differ markedly in appearance. This difference is commonly described as a difference in style. No other aspect of product design can provoke so much discussion as that of style. Logically, it is the least important aspect, coming at the end of the spectrum outlined in Chapter One. Yet it may have a considerable influence upon the product purchaser. This influence is most noticeable in domestic products but it is by no means absent from engineering equipment. On occasions it may seem that style is given more importance than the need for aesthetic pleasure, good ergonomic characteristics or even the attainment of technical requirements. Quite frequently it is possible to identify features which do not contribute to more important requirements. Indeed these so-called styling features may well prevent these requirements from being fully realised. The automobile has often been criticised in this respect and, no doubt, will go on being criticised as long as so many people regard it as an expression of themselves as much as a means for getting from one place to another.

Engineers either indulge in interminable arguments on style or endeavour to ignore it since it appears to serve no useful purpose. In both cases they suspect that unpredictable changes are mischievously produced by somewhat superficially minded stylists. Further they may assert that to change a product purely for the sake of appearances may seem indefensible particularly when, as is the case with some types of consumer product, such changes may occur at fairly frequent intervals. But while changes of this kind may be criticised, it must be pointed out that if any product is to be effective at all, it must be sold by its maker. If style influences sales then clearly it cannot be ignored. And there is ample evidence that—certainly in the field of consumer product design: cars, cookers and so on—style affects sales.

At the present time there is a tendency among some industrial designers to deplore what they describe as styling but at the same time they readily build characteristics into their own designs which they have taken from other types of product. In doing this they have, in effect, been concerned with style. Depending upon the type of product whose characteristics they have embodied, they have also worked in an entirely valid manner. This point will be appreciated in the following analysis of the component influences in the development and life of any particular style. But in relation to a current use of 'styling' in a somewhat derogatory manner, it is probably more true to say that there is good styling and bad styling. Some designers and design critics tend to suggest that good styling implies an absence of super-fluous features in that all the characteristics in a product are formed either in a manner best suited to its use or to production requirements. Bad styling implies the incorporation of 'non-functional' features or components. There are two drawbacks to this generalisation. The first is that in many cases there is no 'best' solution. The second is that the history of product design overflows with examples of the incor-poration of so-called non-functional features. One may feel that this interpretation of the difference between good and bad styling is very largely conditioned by our modern 'functionalist' style which developed in the early twentieth century. Recalling the expression 'form follows function', a U.S. industrial designer recently suggested an interesting modification, namely 'form *permits* function'. For those who find functional styles impersonal and clinical, this suggestion may well have some appeal. But it might be anathema to die-hard 'functionalists' who see it ushering in superfluous features which in the foregoing interpretation, would be regarded as bad styling.

A more generous view, particularly bearing in mind the history of product design, would be that good styling arranges all elements in a design, whether non-functional or otherwise, in a manner which gives aesthetic pleasure; bad styling does not. This may allow for a measure of ornamentation but it does not imply that a product, completely obscured by decorative media, though in a balanced or harmonious manner, would necessarily give aesthetic pleasure. The need to discern a product's purpose, described in Section 5.3, together with the effect of the environment and the designer's own style would tend to qualify this rather more liberal attitude to 'styling'.

6.1 THE COMPONENTS OF STYLE

6.1.1 BASIC FACTORS

A fundamental feature of all the significant styles in the history of product design is that these styles were derived from any or all of three main developments:

1. Finding new ways of achieving technical requirements.
2. Using new materials, and
3. New methods of manufacture.

Perhaps architecture provides the finest field for studying the effect, or usually the interacting effect, of each of these aspects. The Greeks developed the column and beam system of construction to a very refined degree and in doing so established a style which has been perpetuated, though frequently in an adulterated fashion, right up to present times. Gothic architecture bases its characteristic style very largely on the development of the pointed arch, while a large modern building may display a more rectilinear form whenever construction is based upon a skeletal framework of rolled steel sections. In the latter case the method of construction emerged from the introduction of a new type of material and this aspect has been a frequent cause of a change in style, particularly in engineering.

In present day engineering the influences of the three basic factors—technical, material and constructional—can be readily detected. In much production machinery, the application of electronic control systems, which are best housed in box-like casings, has encouraged a development of rectilinear machine forms. Where steel plate fabrication has replaced cast construction, rectilinear forms have been further encouraged. Here of course, changes in material and method of construction are linked together. If and when new techniques, new materials and new methods of manufacture are introduced, then this rectilinear characteristic may well be changed or, at least modified. For example, the increasing use of plastics on machine casings could introduce, or perhaps revive, more curvaceous forms. However, while the three foregoing aspects are the prime factors in any change in style, and should always be looked for in changes to engineering products, they are by no means the only factors. The environment can also have a powerful influence on product style.

6.1.2 THE ENVIRONMENTAL FACTOR

As noted in Chapter Five part of an aesthetic reaction depends not only upon the nature of the product itself but also upon its visual relationship with its surroundings. The person who buys a fifteenth-century house may wish to fill it with faked fifteenth-century furniture since the genuine articles may be hard to obtain. Though he may have some difficulty with telephones and television sets, he is at least responding to the environmental factor; a response which everyone feels either consciously or subconsciously.

Undoubtedly the greatest environmental influence has been that of architecture since it has so often formed the setting for many types of product. Throughout the history of product design, particularly that of domestic products, links with architectural forms can be noted. The relationship may be one of proportion or in the continuation of decorative media. On occasions it may even come from choosing similar materials and fashioning them in a similar manner. The Greeks achieved a strong sense of environmental unity by using proportioning systems such as the Golden Ratio system and also by the continuity of decorative devices. When the Gothic style of building was revived in the nineteenth century, similar characteristics were built into products, sometimes to an almost ludicrous degree. The acanthus leaf, a favourite decorative device, wandered through the plaster of buildings, across the wood of furniture and even into the cast-iron frames of the emerging machines.

Today rectilinear buildings have helped to encourage the design of rectilinear products. In this context the relationship may not be simply aesthetic but also one of making the best use of available space. Storage devices whether for clothes, tableware or kitchen utensils now have box-like forms partly for this reason. Perhaps a striking example of linking products with architecture is show by le Corbusier's 'Modulor' proportioning system. Based on the Golden Ratio and using human dimensions as reference bases, the Modulor was conceived for domestic products as well as for the structures into which they are fitted.

It may be felt that the foregoing applies primarily to the domestic world and that it has little to do with engineering equipment. But in life, the human world cannot be neatly divided into compartments. The impressions acquired from one sort of environment inevitably influence attitudes to others. Even some of the earliest power machinery shows characteristics carried over from other fields of design. A Greek-columned beam engine, scroll-formed cast frames on textile machinery and the ubiquitous acanthus leaf are nineteenth-century examples of the effect of what might be called a living environment upon a working environment. At the present time this influence is increasing, partly due to a greater concern with human welfare in working environments and partly as more tasks are automated. Since a living environment normally evokes feelings of security and comfort it is entirely reasonable that at least some of its characteristics should be carried through into a working environment. And where operators have sedentary occupations which nevertheless involve a higher mental load, as may be the case with complex automated plant, then there is even more justification for the increasing effect of the living world upon the working world. But while this influence may be architecturally based, yet other factors are involved.

6.1.3 SOCIAL FACTORS

While architecture may be given a leading place among the environmental influences on product style, its styles have not always emerged from new technical solutions, new materials or methods of construction. It may be argued that, until the nineteenth century when iron came into use in structures, the last significant architectural development was the Gothic system of construction. But from the true Gothic period up to the twentieth century when the use of new materials and methods became more obvious, there were quite distinct variations in style. Such styles as nineteenth-century Gothic and eighteenth-century classicism resulted from social rather than

material causes. Eighteenth-century architecture modelled on Greek
classical styles developed in part from a revived interest in Greek and
Roman periods. This interest was, of course, confined to the ruling
or upper classes which throughout history have set their stamp on
architecture and product design. While the leadership of ruling classes
bareley exists today, other forms of leadership have taken its place.
To some degree it may be argued that society is now more impressed
by products which are regarded as superior rather than by people who
have acquired or been invested with superior positions. For example,
the development of aircraft produced streamlined forms which very
quickly found their way into products which needed no aerodynamic
consideration whatsoever. A sharpening of line in the modern aircraft has led to a sharpening of line in other types of product, even
though there is no aerodynamic necessity for such a modification. The
aircraft was regarded as 'advanced' and consequently influenced the
form of other products. At the moment, after a short flirtation with
forms culled from imaginary space-ships, (the real craft having little
relationship to the imagined), there is a tendency to revere devices
such as computers and controls for automated plant. Thus products
such as cookers may be found which, while embodying more controls
in terms of setting and timing devices, nevertheless give a computer-
like impression. Such styles usually apply to consumer products and
have a comparatively short life. But they certainly provide an example
of the way society may influence style by way of what it takes to be
a 'leader'.

Besides being influenced by leaders, whether human or material,
society may aspire to a certain way of life. This may also affect
product style. While these aspirations have often been encouraged
by individuals, a number of cases might be cited where a general
movement towards different standards of living has occurred. In some
cases such developments may be comparatively short-lived. As
mentioned in Section 4.7.4, after the Second World War there was a
movement towards more colourful products as a reaction to the
enforced drabness of the war period. This lasted for roughly a decade
moving away to what we regard at the moment as a more subtle use
of colour. While in terms of the life of some products this trend was
comparatively short-lived, other trends may carry over a longer
period. An ancillary influence in the more clinical form of early

twentieth-century products was undoubtedly a greater concern with public and personal cleanliness. The expression 'clean-looking' is still an indication of approbation. Another indication of the influence of social aspirations and ways of life can be found by noting differences in products made in different countries. What is commonly called the internationalisation of design is as much due to an approaching equivalence in aspiring to a particular way of life (though it may by no means have been achieved), as it is to equivalence of production methods.

It may be argued that those who produce new forms and colours which are not based upon more fundamental aspects of style, are themselves acting as leaders. Everyone, so the argument runs, would be quite content with what they have if it were not for those who with massive publicity, force the 'latest' upon a submissive public. But, by and large, it is likely that people cannot be gulled quite so easily. They may not accept changes unless these changes relate with their attitudes and aspirations. In clothing, where style plays a leading role, the successful designers are those who are, as it were, in touch with life and able to give it visual expression. Modern clothes underline the greater mobility and less formal patterns of living which many people now enjoy. Then, most people grow accustomed to the shape of things around them. In the field of product design, many designers agree that it is not possible to make sudden and pronounced changes. So-called traditional characteristics may be sustained, not because they have any intrinsic merit but simply because they are familiar. The establishment of stereotypes noted in Section 5.3 may be recalled in this context.

The passage of one style into another often demonstrates a desire to retain the familiar even though moving forward to new concepts. Thus in architecture features such as Greek columns were often retained though they might have no structural purpose. In engineering, particularly in transport, the features of earlier types of vehicle have been built into newer devices very largely because of their familiarity. However, it is only fair to point out that while completely novel concepts may be suspected, they do not occur as frequently as may be imagined. Progress in product design has, more often than not, an evolutionary character which also tends to merge one style with another.

To round off this survey of social influences on product design, reference must be made to so-called status seeking. At present this aspect is often treated with a certain cynicism if not with outright derision. But it has existed, in one form or another, throughout history. It may be recalled from Chapter One that the expression 'status symbol' can be shown to have a literal origin. Today products do not so much embody literal symbols as become symbolic in themselves. Psychological studies under the title of *Motivational Research* have purported to show that people buy products for other reasons than their ability to perform particular tasks. The Rolls-Royce car is a superb piece of engineering but it is also a symbol of affluence. Yet status does not necessarily imply seeking an appearance if not the reality of affluence, for today affluence is by no means the only social goal. Much modern advertising endeavours to impress the potential customer not only with the merits of the product but also with the happy, carefree, or exciting life its fictional owners appear to be having. Many people are not as immune to this type of approach as they may believe. And even if they do not accept the advertiser's symbolisms they may very well have a number of their own. To condemn manufacturers for trading upon these attitudes, by making comparatively frequent changes to certain types of product, is to condemn them for being aware of human traits which have demonstrably existed for a very long time. Certainly the changes may be of a quite ephemeral character contributing little to the mainstreams of social development and, at base, unrelated to technical, material or production factors. But, if one takes a liberal view of this kind of ephemeral styling, and it must be pointed out that not everyone does, one should certainly expect more fundamental design requirements to have been achieved. Unfortunately, all too frequently, this is not the case. For example 'fashionable' materials and 'distinctive' control features on an automobile facia should be roundly condemned when they prove unsuitable in ergonomic terms.

Sometimes there are complaints that all too frequently styling idioms are reproduced in products other than those for which they were first created. During the 1950s when tail fins began to adorn many automobiles, other products also began to sprout these pseudo-aerodynamic stabilisers. While this generally occurs in consumer product design, capital equipment has not been entirely immune from the effect of short-lived idioms. Taking a liberal attitude towards status symbolism and the short-lived styles it encourages, then this might be acceptable. However capital equipment must usually last for a much longer period than most consumer products. Consequently the embodiment of short-lived idioms will almost certainly create a dated if not an incongruous appearance after several years have passed.

There is no quick and easy guide either to forecasting future styles or to estimating which current styles may be regarded as valid and which have only a temporary significance. While much of the foregoing applies to consumer products, there is, as noted earlier, no sharply divided approach to the products forming our environment. Later on, a guide for capital equipment designers is proposed but it cannot be regarded as more than a suggestion. The best guide is an awareness of changes in products other than those with which the engineering designer is concerned coupled with an understanding of how these changes are caused. But before reaching this point, there is another aspect of style which can be reasonably connected with status-seeking attitudes. This is concerned with the status sought by the manufacturer rather than that sought by his potential customer. It is generally referred to as 'house-style', though other expressions, notably 'corporate identity' have been used.

6.2 HOUSE STYLE

Just as a person may in part be judged by his appearance, so a manufacturer may be judged by the appearance of all he produces. If his products appear out-of-date, badly finished or crude and ungainly, these characteristics may detract from the impression he may wish to make upon his markets. And this impression will be built up, not only from the appearance of his products, but also from the appearance of his catalogues, advertisements, stationery, exhibition equipment, delivery vehicles and also his premises.

If a good aesthetic standard can be maintained in all these features, it is likely that they will have a stimulating influence upon the manufacturer's personnel as well as upon his potential customers. An impression will be given that the manufacturer really cares about the things he produces. But further, if there can be clear visual links in products, trade literature and so on, the manufacturer is more likely to be regarded as operating in a well-planned manner. This visual continuity will make him more readily discernible in his markets; an aspect which can be especially important to manufacturers trading over long distances. A first impression made upon potential customers may well be through the visual impression made by catalogues or displays in trade exhibitions. Subsequently there will come the impressions made by products, by correspondence and by instruction and service manuals.

Another approach to the subject of house style is to recognise that a manufacturer is not just selling products. To be more precise he is providing a service. His products are simply one part of the service he offers to those with whom he is trading. Other parts may be the assistance he offers his customer in matters of purchase, delivery, installation, operation and maintenance. Thus, if the means he uses for providing this service have a good and well-related aesthetic standard, then he will be more highly regarded. This approach explains the concern with house style shown by transport organisations such as shipping-lines, airlines and railways. In such cases there is no product and the concept of providing a service becomes clearer. It also tends to become more noticeable in cases where the product has either very little visual character in itself, i.e. materials such as steel or oil, tea, sugar etc.; or where products may have a comparatively standardised form, i.e. engineering components such as ball bearings, pipe couplings, nuts and bolts.

6.2.1 POTENTIAL COMMON STANDARDS IN A HOUSE STYLE

Perhaps the most significant influence in a house style results from using standardised letter forms and layouts. Choosing lettering and lettering layout which can be clearly seen, understood and applicable to all the manufacturer produces is by no means an easy task. Where engineering products are involved it may be necessary to select letter forms and to design layouts which can be reproduced in cast form on the machinery, by etching or screen printing on instruction labels, and by normal printing techniques on catalogues, service manuals and so on. Lettering and layout should also be distinctive particularly in relation to that of competitors. Further and particularly in engineering, it should not be likely to go out of date. Finally it should help to express the type of service which the manufacturer is providing. For example, if he is producing very refined equipment, there should be a sense of refinement in letter and layout design.

In order to register his identity a manufacturer may well use a symbol or trade-mark. Simplicity, the ability to be reproduced in a variety of forms and of a character which expresses the manufacturer's purpose, are necessary ingredients of good symbol design. Clearly there must be no likelihood of confusion with other symbols. However, though this may be contested, the search for 'unique' symbols can be overdone. If a manufacturers' name is short and distinctive, or can be abbreviated, using initials, a symbol may not be necessary.

Colour standardisation can strongly support a house style; though in engineering, colour selection should be determined by its ergonomic quality as described in Chapter Five. It is an advantage if colours can be distinctive but this advantage may be effected by selecting distinctive combinations of standard colours rather than by endeavouring to produce special colours. It may be necessary to make a thorough investigation of meanings attached to colours in those markets with which the manufacturer is concerned, otherwise the manufacturer may run the risk of inhibiting rather than stimulating his potential customers.

Where products of a similar type but different capacity (e.g. electric motors or pumps etc.), are being provided or where products combine to provide a common service (e.g. a business accounting system or a material processing plant), then standardisation of machine forms is most valuable. This standardisation should carry through to control components, the manner in which these components are arranged, control and instruction lettering and methods used to fit such services as electric conduit, hydraulic and pneumatic piping. These latter features may well be overlooked and, on last minute and uninstructed installation, may completely ruin all that has gone before.

6.2.2 ESSENTIAL REQUIREMENTS FOR A SOUND HOUSE STYLE

A house style can only be developed with strong management support and by co-operation between those departmental heads who will apply it. These will usually be the heads of design, production, marketing and publicity sections, who may have to meet at intervals in order to ensure that standards are being maintained. Deterioration can easily occur if this is not done. Company standards books incorporating house style requirements help to support a consistent approach. But care must be taken to ensure that the standards laid down are sufficiently flexible to cope with envisaged variations whether in the products or in publicity material. Besides encouraging a sound house style, standardisation should encourage economies and these may be quite significant particularly in large organisations where purchase and production orders may be made by a variety of personnel.

Another essential requirement is that a house style should be comprehensive. A partial approach, say by simply producing a symbol and title, will not have so great an influence either in a company's markets or among its personnel. Indeed it may be more confusing, especially if other systems of identification are employed. If a house style is being introduced, then there is bound to be a period of transition. But this period should be kept as short as is economically possible. In general, the quickest and most economic way is to deal with stationery, catalogues, advertisements, and name-plates. But care must be taken that techniques devised for these items can be carried through to all else which a company produces or by which it is identified.

Finally a house style should tell the truth. It should be an honest expression of the type of service being provided by a manufacturer. A house style may register the status of a manufacturer but it will not, in itself, create one for him. Indeed if the service he provides is either inadequate or inefficient, a house style may well become a liability rather than a symbol of repute. A current good example of a house style is shown in Plate 6.1.

6.3 OBSERVING STYLE IN CAPITAL GOODS

Most items of capital plant and equipment have to function for periods over which styles in consumer product design may change considerably. Therefore, it is important that capital goods should not be encumbered with devices of a comparatively ephemeral nature.

First and foremost in capital goods, style should emerge from the way the product is devised in order to perform its task coupled with the way in which it is made. Referring to the spectrum analogy, style should be based upon all the factors to the left of its position in the spectrum and linked to the framework within which this spectrum of requirements has to be met.

In what might be called the aesthetic area of this spectrum, the concept of purpose is of special importance. The nature of the function which the machine has to perform and its constructional quality should be clearly visible. This, as pointed out in Chapter Five, does not always happen in the solution of technical and manufacturing problems.

The foregoing aspects are by far the most important in determining or assessing style in the design of capital goods. However, a relationship with modern characteristics in other types of product can be of value if carefully treated. The danger here lies in copying characteristics which either do not supplement the need to clearly delineate 'purpose' or which are of a comparatively shortlived nature. An assessment of a product's relationship with modern architectural forms provides the safest approach because architecture usually has a longer life and often acts as the frame within which a product is seen. Consumer products, with their comparatively short working lives, are likely to be misleading.

A final assessment of style in capital goods can be made by seeing how well the product displays its maker's house style. Here the assessment depends not only upon the incorporation of characteristics which will clearly identify the maker but also upon whether these characteristics signify the quality of the maker's service.

In conclusion, though taking all precautions to ensure that so-called styling devices are omitted, it will be found that even capital goods will appear to become 'dated' after a number of years have passed. This is because there are bound to be changes in methods of achieving technical requirements coupled with changes in methods of manufacture. But when this occurs it is usually time to change the product in the total sense. To appear to do so by attempting to apply an up-to-date style to an out-of-date mechanism is to be guilty of deceit.

Chapter Seven

INDUSTRIAL DESIGN
IN PRACTICE

7.1 THE GENERAL DESIGN SITUATION

IN Chapter One, industrial design in engineering was explained in terms of dealing with human responses to industrial products. These responses have been shown to cover ergonomic responses, aesthetic responses and, perhaps more nebulous in character, responses to style. It has also been shown that these three aspects of product design are interlinked and that they could be visualised as forming part of a spectrum; the spectrum of industrial design. This spectrum is by no means isolated from the technical aspects of design. The so-called technical and human aspects merge together, particularly in meeting ergonomic requirements. Moreover, the extent to which all requirements can be achieved must be conditioned by those materials, skills and manufacturing resources which are available.

In practice, the availability of materials, skills and manufacturing resources is conditioned by those in the possession of the manufacturer, together with those he is financially able to develop or to call upon. If he were establishing his business on the basis of a particular product design and were financially able to do so, the manufacturer would acquire those resources which he believed appropriate to its production. However, the usual case is that he already possesses materials (or more often the ability to purchase materials), skills in terms of design capacity and manufacturing 'know-how', and manufacturing resources in terms of machine tools or other forms of production equipment. His products must therefore be suited to these resources which he must use in as economical a manner as possible. Thus he must not waste material and he must make the most of the 'know-how' and manufacturing equipment which either he possesses or which he is able to call upon. Usually, a manufacturer's resources do not just affect the extent to which all requirements are achieved in a product they very largely determine the type of product he will make.

Clearly, a manufacturer will not make a product which he feels is not a saleable proposition. Thus while deciding upon a product which suits those resources available to him, he must make a thorough study of those markets in which his product is likely to be purchased. In a large number of cases he will find that other manufacturers are producing similar goods. He then has to consider whether he can make his product superior to all others in every respect or whether he can achieve superiority in one or several aspects which, in his view, will appeal to the markets at which he is aiming. At first sight, some of these aspects may not appear to have any direct bearing upon product design. For example the manufacturer might believe that he can surpass his competitors if he is able to deliver his product more quickly. But depending upon the nature of the product, this might be achieved by designing standardised units and embodying as many standard components as is possible. Thus a stock of units could be built up to permit speedy assembly or speedy transport in unit form with assembly at the customer's site. In fact there are very few aspects in the whole trading situation which in one form or another do not influence the way in which a product is designed. Even the manner in which the product is sold, whether by direct sale, through agents, or on short or long term credit, can influence product design. While in theory the ideal selling situation would be one in which the manu-facturer surpassed his competitor in every conceivable respect, in practice this is seldom possible. Indeed certain aspects are likely to be in apparent conflict. For example, it might seem advantageous to sell a product with a proven long service life. But to do this the manu-facturer might require to use stronger materials and more refined manufacturing techniques than those of his competitors and this may make his product more expensive. Therefore in practice, the extent to which all requirements in a product are achieved also depends upon the manufacturer's judgement of what will appeal to his envisaged markets, particularly in relation to his competitors. In addition to aspects which are recognisably part of the product, this may extend to what are commonly called trading aspects, but as noted these too will usually have some bearing on the way the product is designed.

The assessment of what is possible with available resources and the judgement of market conditions will or should, in practice, be undertaken together. In modern engineering management, or indeed in the management of other forms of business, combined assessment of available resources and market situations becomes increasingly important, and may call for the use of refined techniques in order to obtain sufficient information upon which decisions can be taken. This is particularly the case where products are of a complex nature, require considerable investment to develop and manufacture or must compete against other products with comparatively marginal advantages. Since situations are constantly changing, such combined assessments must be frequently undertaken. It may be noted that while it is imperative that a product should perform its basic functions (for example an electric motor must give a prescribed power at a specified speed), few business failures occur because the product does not 'work'. Failures may occur because the product does not work as well as those of competitors, but quite frequently failures occur because either the manufacturer has misjudged the market situation, producing a product which has no appeal though it may be an excellent piece of engineering, or because he has chosen to make something which while having 'market appeal' is beyond his resources.

7.2 SPECIFYING DESIGN REQUIREMENTS

The expression 'design policy' is commonly used to refer to the group of decisions which will determine the type of goods produced by a manufacturer and the manner in which his various requirements are incorporated in them. A design policy will cover other aspects such as the way design work is organised and the facilities provided for undertaking design work. However, direction on the type of products which a company intends to manufacture and the qualities which they are intended to possess form the basis of a design policy. A manufacturer will naturally wish to impress his envisaged markets with those qualities which be believes are superior to those of his competitors. Thus,

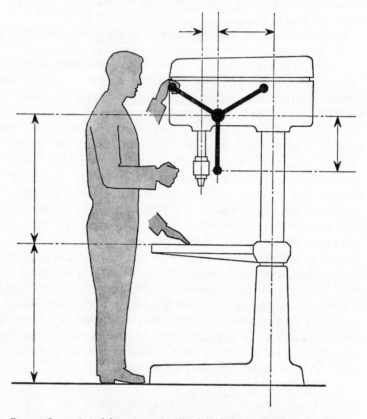

FIG. 7.1 *Some principal dimensions on a pillar drill which may be different according to the design policy adopted by the maker. Will he aim for maximum operator convenience or maximum drilling capacity? In practice a compromise will be sought but, even so, there can be differences of emphasis*

where he may not be able to achieve an overall lead, he will seek to establish a reputation for one or more qualities which he regards as advantageous. At the same time he cannot overlook qualities in his competitors' products which, while not regarded as so important as those upon which he is establishing his reputation, nevertheless must be embodied in his own product. For example he may pin his faith on providing a product with the greatest possible capacity for undertaking a particular duty. Another manufacturer may decide to produce a similar product with the greatest possible operating convenience. The drill in Fig. 7.1 shows the main dimensions influencing machine capacity in relation to operator convenience. It is more than likely that if one drill were designed with maximum conceivable capacity in mind and another with the best possible operating convenience in mind, the two drills would be distinctly different in respect of these dimensions. However because operating convenience is important in itself and because a competitor may place emphasis upon it, it must obviously be taken into account. Clearly in practice, a measure of so-called compromise will be reached.

A design policy describing the nature of those products which a manufacturer intends to make and emphasising those qualities which he feels give him distinct advantages in the market, forms the foundation for design specifications. A clear and comprehensive design specification is of vital importance. Inadequate specifications may, at worst, cause market failures and, at best, extend product development time when, on producing a prototype, some qualities may be found to be not as good as they might have been. Attempts to graft on improvements to the product, often somewhat hurriedly, can seldom be successful. Not only is more time and money consumed, but also these improvements cannot be embodied as well as if the qualities to which they relate had been recognised in the first instance. It cannot be too often repeated that design work is essentially a process of synthesis, of bringing together a number of requirements to make a corporate whole. If requirements are overlooked then the resultant product is bound to be incomplete.

Bearing in mind the general situation under which design work is undertaken, a specification *must* give information which will either directly or indirectly define those resources available for product design. Usually the information is indirect in the sense that available resources are determined by quoting desirable product costs, envisaged quantities and desirable design, development and manufacturing periods. Thus if development has to be achieved within a certain period of time, materials which may take a longer period to obtain could clearly not be used. Similarly materials and processes which would increase cost beyond the envisaged figure would also be excluded. Determination of permissible costs and development times in design specifications makes it important that production costs— generally in terms of labour, material (including purchased components), and overhead costs—should be known by the designer. He also needs to know how long the various processes of development and production are likely to take. Perhaps in an earlier period a designer would acquire this information by experience, particularly where the product was made almost entirely by the manufacturer's own facilities. But in modern engineering practice with the increased complexity of production processes and the use of other manufacturers facilities either by sub-contract or in the purchase of components, it becomes important to constantly 'feed' designers with current costs and cost breakdowns. When this is done, a framework within which design work must be undertaken can be more readily determined.

While determination of cost, quantity, development and manufacturing time form an important part of any specification, it is likely that this information will be preceded by basic performance requirements, safety requirements and any other requirements which are called for by national or international standards. This group of requirements might be classed as essentials in any design specification. Obviously the product must work and work within any regulations laid down to cover safety and aspects such as period of service and quality of materials and manufacture. In many cases a manufacturer may wish to establish his reputation on one or several aspects of basic performance. In production machinery for example, he may seek to increase operating speeds in order to increase output. Perhaps other manufacturers may not wish to go quite so far, though they well recognise that an increase in operating speed will increase output. However, they may assert that quality matters as much as quantity and feel that faster speeds may create inaccuracies in production. Faster speeds might also mean more frequent maintenance or the installation of more complex equipment in order to help keep the machine running. All this depends, of course, upon the product under consideration and should not be regarded as a general fact. But if certain parts of the essential requirements in a design specification go to support the reputation a manufacturer is seeking, then they will or should be emphasised.

A specification will certainly include other matters. Depending upon the nature of the product, aspects such as packaging, storage, transport, installation, maintenance, after sales service, quality, interchangeability, and use of standard components and products, will also be noted. There may also be details concerning trading aspects such as delivery periods, when these aspects are considered to have, as they often will, a bearing on the way the product is designed. Thus with the foregoing in mind it is now possible to consider those aspects falling within the spectrum of industrial design.

7.3 RATING THE IMPORTANCE OF INDUSTRIAL DESIGN

When encouraging interest in any particular department of the whole design spectrum, it is tempting to imply that it is of the greatest importance. However it would be irresponsible to suggest that this was so with industrial design factors. There would be little point in producing a good-looking product which did not meet basic performance and safety requirements. Taking the simple spectrum outlined in Chapter One, it can be said that for *any* type of product embodying the factors in this spectrum, technical aspects will be more important than ergonomic aspects and ergonomic aspects more important than aesthetic aspects. Taking, for example, a piece of furnishing fabric, in which there is certainly little ergonomic content apart from being of a size and form which can be manipulated, it may well be that this product will be bought entirely because of its pleasing appearance. But if it fades, shrinks or deteriorates due to wear or for any other reason then, however pleasing the appearance, the product cannot be regarded as well designed in the complete sense in which this expression should be used. In this regard it may be worth pointing out that the ideal design improvement would be one which, as it were, elevates the excellence of all factors in the design spectrum, without enlarging, indeed preferably contracting, the framework of those resources within which the product must be produced. On occasions this may be overlooked by those wishing to encourage improvement in one or other design factor. Considerable confusion can be caused when products are judged by attempting to treat factors in isolation. It must be repeated that design is concerned with the integration of *all* factors and that *all* factors are interconnected to a greater or lesser extent. Judgements of partial aspects are certainly useful for illustrative or educational purposes. But they can be extremely misleading to those who do not have or do not need to have knowledge of all that is involved in design work. On occasions such judgements may also be highly irritating, especially for those dealing with the most important factors, when factors of lesser importance are singled out for approbation without apparent recognition of design realities.

However, a grading of importance does not, of course, imply that factors of lesser importance can be either overlooked or treated in a negligent manner. Thus those coming within the spectrum of industrial design should be covered in any design specification and their importance should be rated against the importance of other factors. While in the general situation it can be said that they are less important than basic performance requirements, it is obviously useful to assess by how much they are of lesser or greater importance than other requirements. Though techniques which endeavour to produce quantitative assessments of relative values are developing, it is doubtful whether precise gradations of value can ever be achieved. This is largely because a manufacturer would have to be absolutely certain that the product qualities upon which he wished to concentrate would be entirely successful in the market. Unfortunately he can never be absolutely sure. Furthermore changing market conditions and changes in the resources available to him may very well force him to change his scale of values. Yet though it may not be possible to make precise quantitative judgements, it is convenient to form some kind of picture of the relative values. This might be done in a variety of ways but since the analogy of a spectrum contained by a framework of resources has been used to the moment, it will be convenient to continue to use it.

Fig. 7.2 shows the expanded spectra for two types of product. These design requirements are entirely hypothetical and do not

Products which have improved in other ways besides appearance. They represent the ideal of always attempting to make 'overall' design improvements. In all cases they represent the result of good team work by all engaged in the design task.

(i)

PLATES 7.1(a) Electrocardiograph. Maker: Cambridge Instrument Co. Ltd. Consultant industrial designer: F. C. Ashford. A product improved in performance, less costly to make, easier to handle and operate, and better looking. (i)—Before improvement, (ii)—After improvement (Photographs: Courtesy of the Cambridge Instrument Co. Ltd.)

(ii)

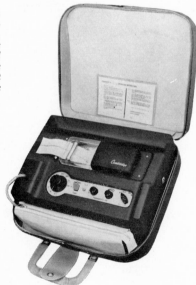

PLATE 7.1(b) *Inclinable press. Maker: Horden, Mason & Edwards Ltd. Consultant industrial designers: Allen-Bowden Ltd. This machine embodies a more refined control system, is structurally stiffer as well as better looking than its predecessors. Note the use of colour to increase apparent base mass (Photograph: R. W. Brown, Birmingham)*

(ii)

(i)

PLATE 7.1(c) *Industrial Boiler. Maker: Thomas Petterton. Consultant industrial designers: E. Marshall & Associates. Heat transfer characteristics and production techniques are improved as well as appearance.* (i)—*Before improvement,* (ii)—*After improvement* (Photographs: C.o.I.D.)

PLATE 7.1(d) *Test Meter. Maker: Wayne Kerr Ltd. Consultant industrial designers: London & Upjohn. This unit is part of a range (Photograph: C.o.I.D.)*

(i)

(ii)

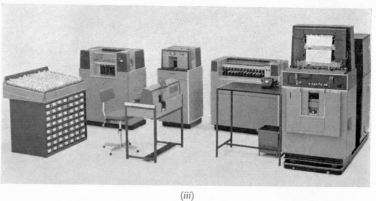

(iii)

PLATES 7.1(e) *Card punch unit, part of the accounting system shown in (iii). (i)—Before improvement (Photograph: Studio Cole Ltd.), (ii)—After improvement (Photograph: Studio Briggs). Unit easier to make while relating visually the other units in the system, (iii)—Complete accounting system (Photograph: Peter Waugh). Maker: International Computers and Tabulators (I.C.T.)*

(iv)

(v)

PLATE 7.1(e) (Continued:) (iv)—1900 Series computer system in which the computer itself is considerably reduced in size compared with predecessors. (v)—Enlargement of part of the system showing refined attention to details which enhances precision qualities. Maker: International Computers and Tabulators (I.C.T.) (Photographs: Peter Waugh)

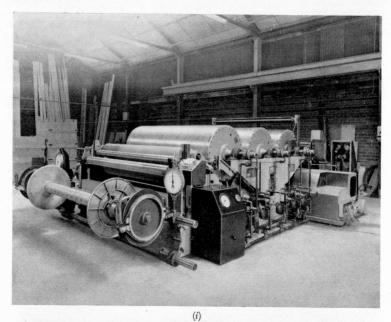

(i)

(ii)

PLATE 7.1(f) *Textile warp sizing machine. Maker: Leesona Ltd. Consultant industrial designers: Allen-Bowden Ltd. More refined control systems are embodied in the improved unit. (i)—An earlier sizing machine, (ii)—An improved version (Photographs: Courtesy of Leesona Holt Ltd., Heywood, Lancs.)*

PLATE 7.1(g) *Excavator. Maker: Peter Hamilton Equipment Ltd. Consultant industrial designers: Douglas Scott Associates. Improved in capacity and in ease of control, as well as visually. Note, lack of excrescence so common in this type of equipment (Photograph: William Tribe Ltd.)*

PLATE 7.1 (h) *Film type-setting machine. Maker: The Monotype Corporation Ltd. Consultant industrial designers: Wilkes and Ashmore. There is no predecessor. The product represents an 'ideal' in that the appearance and ease of use were taken into account throughout the development.*
(Photograph by courtesy of The Monotype Corporation Ltd.)

PLATE 7.1 (*i*)
(*Photograph: Courtesy of The Colchester Lathe Company*)

Centre-lathe. Maker: The Colchester Lathe Company. Consultant industrial designer: F. C. Ashford. Designed for manufacture by production-line techniques. This machine represents an ideal in terms of teamwork. Ergonomic research (by the Ergonomics Dept. Cranfield College of Aeronautics) provided an improved feed chart, to be incorporated by engineering designers and the industrial designer. Note how style does not follow the current rectangular idiom but is based on functional and material requirements—e.g. the shape of the headstock end housing is well suited to its material (which is glass fibre)

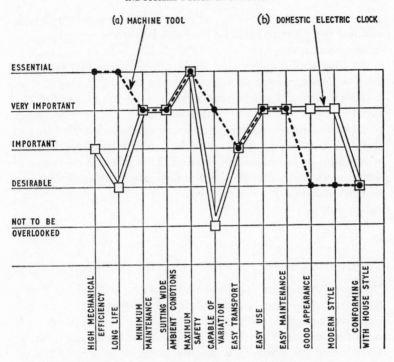

FIG. 7.2 *Spectra of requirements for two sorts of product, (a) a machine tool and (b) a domestic clock. A grading of* RELATIVE *importance, as suggested, helps to decide how design work should be biassed—but clearly all requirements must be taken into account. Note that in practice the identification of* ALL *requirements is an important task*

include all that may be relevant. Product (*a*) is assumed to be a piece of manufacturing equipment, such as a machine tool, operating for long periods under continuous human control. It is made in comparatively small quantities and the manufacturer wishes to establish a reputation for selling durable equipment requiring a minimum of maintenance. His spectrum is likely to appear as shown though it must be emphasised that it will be conditioned by other makers. Thus while he has not apparently set his sights at, say, attractive appearance he cannot lag behind other manufacturers. Product (*b*) is assessed to be a consumer product, such as a domestic electric clock, handled at infrequent intervals, and with a fairly long life. It is made in quantity and the manufacturer wishes to establish a reputation for accuracy of performance and attractive appearance. His spectrum may well be as outlined though once again he must not lag behind competitors in other respects.

By using semi-diagrammatic, semi-pictorial concepts for rating the relative importance of all relevant design factors, it may not be possible to arrive at precise ratings but it is possible to note that one factor is, say, very much more important, or a little more important or of equivalent importance in relation to any other. Such devices are also useful in that they can be used to show the range of requirements which must be met in the final product. Thus when, in the course of design work, the inevitable 'compromises' are being dealt with, the designer can bias his design towards meeting the manufacturer's design policy.

7.4 INDUSTRIAL DESIGN IN THE DESIGN PROCESS

Whatever importance is given to ergonomic, aesthetic and style factors one of the great skills in design is to wring as much from one's resources as possible, making as it were advances on all fronts while supporting the manufacturer's reputation. For example, Plate 7.1 shows several products which show improvements in most respects over their predecessors. That is, they have improved in basic performance, are easier to operate, look better and are made either as economically, and in some cases more economically than their predecessors. Whatever the product and whatever their rated importance, consideration should be given to industrial design factors from the start of design work. Quite frequently and particularly when a new operating principle is likely to be used, experimental models may be produced first. In some cases, the design of an experimental model has to concentrate entirely upon performance requirements especially where the operating principle is highly original. But once basic principles have been proven *all* design factors should be considered from the outset of the design project.

The design process has been described in various ways by writers on design and the following outline is only one of several descriptions, all of which follow the same general course. This outline has the merit of simplicity and is as follows:

1. It is first necessary to define the problem and this in practice means producing a clear and comprehensive specification. It has been seen that, in stating the problem, some ordering of importance should be given to the various requirements since all design problems are composite in the sense that several, indeed usually many, problems have to be solved while being interrelated to produce a corporate whole.

2. The problem statement will be analysed to see just what all requirements involve and how they are likely to relate with one another.

3. Preliminary concepts in which various factors are brought together will be developed and these will be analysed in relation to how well they meet the problem statement. These concepts will develop, say from rough sketches to preliminary schemes until a synthesis of all factors is reached in a way which should satisfy the problem statement.

4. The final synthesis is presented, say by working drawings and perhaps models, in a manner which will enable manufacture.

In brief, the progress of design runs from problem statement to analysis, to synthesis and then to final presentation. It must be noted that, in practice, these stages merge together. For example, a great deal of design work is often done in the presentation stage of preparing working drawings. In addition the designer is continuously moving backwards and forwards, as it were, between analysis and synthesis. It is this characteristic of designing which, in some cases, has been expanded by other writers. Thus after analysis of requirements, 'preliminary synthesis' may be followed by 're-analysis' or 'test' in the sense that the designer tests an hypothesis against the requirements. Indeed he may well do this literally; having an experimental model manufactured before proceeding further. However, the four stages outlined are sufficient as an outline, provided the extent of the work involved in 'synthesis' is recognised.

7.4.1 ANALYSIS

Since industrial design requirements should be called for in the specification however they are rated, then they will need to be analysed. And this analysis will inevitably lead the designer to form preliminary hypotheses which he will begin to relate with other requirements. To some degree, analysis may be regarded as seeking further information or putting information into forms which are more convenient for him. For example the calculation of torque from a specified power and speed requirement in a motor could be classed as analysis. The statement that the product is to be operated by women and directed mainly to European markets will call for some knowledge of those body dimensions which have to be related to operation. In the case of the motor, information is being re-ordered; while in the case of female European operators, further information is being sought.

Bearing this in mind and recognising that some information in a specification can be used directly, the following questionnaire (Section 7.4.1.1) may apply to a variety of engineering products in relation to industrial design factors. Of course, it may also be useful in preparing specifications.

7.4.1.1 'Market' questions influencing industrial design

1. What are the principal markets being aimed at?
2. What groups of people will use the product? (body dimensions; cultural characteristics such as language; form, colour and texture preferences or aversions; prevailing social attitudes).
3. Where will the product be located? (domestic, public or factory environment; character of surrounding architecture and of other products).
4. How will the product relate with other products? (dimensional relationships if combining in a particular system; methods by which the entire system will be operated; relationships of form, colour and texture).
5. Character of competitors' products?
6. Character of similar products against which the manufacturer is not competing but which may be seen by and thus influence the market areas?
7. Selling methods? (will product be displayed in exhibitions or advertisements so calling for a measure of distinction?).
8. Can the manufacturer's reputation be underlined by product appearance? (i.e. if the manufacturer is selling highly accurate

equipment can the product be made to show accuracy?).

9. Can the 'house style', if any, be built into the product?
10. What changes, if any, are envisaged in the foregoing over the foreseeable life of the product?
11. What national standards affect industrial design aspects?

Before proceeding to questions whose answers will be largely determined by available resources it should be noted that, in relation to Questions 2 and 3, a literal acceptance of conditions as they stand could be highly misleading. For example, it would be ludicrous to build a nineteenth-century appearance into a product because it was destined for a factory built in the nineteenth century.

7.4.1.2 'Production' questions

1. What materials and methods can be used in view of cost, development and production requirements? (Clearly this affects all other factors. Often it is easier to obtain a general assessment of what materials and processes are too expensive.)
2. What items either already designed or in stock may be used?
3. What 'bought-out' items are available which, while meeting technical and ergonomic requirements, will augment product appearance?
4. What 'bought-out' items are needed which may detract from product appearance and require treatment, say by shrouding?
5. What finishes, such as painting or plating are permissible in relation to cost and other requirements?
6. Can 'house-style' standards be incorporated in relation to cost and other requirements?
7. Do requirements for interchangeability of components or main machine units affect industrial design factors?
8. Do maintenance or servicing requirements affect industrial design factors?
9. How will assembly, packaging, storage and delivery requirements affect industrial design factors?
10. What changes, if any, are envisaged over the foreseeable life of the product?

7.4.2 SYNTHESIS

A number of the foregoing questions will or should be re-asked when
the designer reaches the stage of re-analysis or investigation of his
preliminary ideas. At this point he will be assessing the interrelationship of all the factors in his design spectrum, constantly trying to
improve all but recognising that he may have to favour one aspect
more than another according to the manufacturer's design policy. The
more experienced the designer the more this process will go on without resorting to drawings or even to rough sketches. Further, in
practice, an experienced designer will not sit down and say, 'now I will
produce a preliminary hypothesis and having done so, I will check its
suitability'. These two activities seem to go on together and at an
extremely rapid rate. It is most likely that a great deal is accomplished
seemingly without conscious thought. The designer 'absorbs' all the
data set by the problem and may well 'sleep on it' for some time.
Many designers, and indeed other creative people, do this deliberately
after thoroughly immersing themselves in the problem. Then at a
later stage the answer appears to arrive, probably at a most inconvenient moment!

For those beginning design work, this technique is unlikely to yield
appropriate results. Yet, assuming they have creative ability, they may
well produce a considerable number of potential answers; on the
surface perhaps more than the experienced designer. Their problem
is usually to know which of these answers is to be preferred. It is here
that the experienced designer is more successful because the type of
questions laid out in the section on analysis, together with those which
concern the interrelationship of factors are, as it were, built into him.

The foregoing applies to any kind of designer. Only practice can
perfect the designer's ability to conceive and discriminate between
the hypotheses he may develop. And most experienced designers
would agree that in the initial stages of synthesis, the whole thinking
process should be kept as fluid as possible. Ideas should not harden too
quickly into orthographic drawings with their hard pencilled fixity.
The roughest of rough sketches, and plenty of them, is to be preferred.

In relation to industrial design factors, particularly overall appearance, it has been pointed out that a simple concept which the designer
can work towards as a visual ideal can be most valuable. But this

ideal should, quite certainly, not be conceived until all design requirements and their implications have been absorbed by the designer. It is
comparatively easy to produce a whole variety of concepts all of
which are equally good-looking, for there are no bests and worsts in
matters of appearance. A designer could conceivably produce highly
ordered rectangular forms or more fluid moulded forms, obtaining
'unity' through absolute symmetry, by asymmetric balances, by
contrast, continuity of elements and so on. But all these concepts
would be entirely hypothetical. The 'ideal' can only evolve from a
full analysis of design requirements. This is what causes many industrial designers to say that product appearance 'grows out of the
design'. It is also a reason for considering industrial design factors
right at the beginning and not towards the end of a design task.

7.4.3 PRESENTATION

Bearing in mind that design work generally continues into the pre-
paration of working drawings, it is clearly important that the character
and quality of the final design should be maintained. The detail
draughtsmen has an enormous power to make or mar a design even
though a professional industrial designer may be employed in a staff
or consultative capacity. Good proportions or colour treatment can be
totally ruined by inadequate finishes and by inattention to detail.
Many aspects of detail can be dealt with by standardisation, thus not
only preserving appearance requirements but also enabling economical
manufacture. But there are bound to be some features on any machine
which cannot be standardised. In this case, one can only rely on the
draughtsman's sensitivity and his willingness to seek advice in the
interests of producing the best possible product, recognising that he
is an important member of the whole design team.

There is no doubt that pictorial drawings, preferably in colour, can
be of considerable value to both production and marketing sections
in any company. Models, more finished than those which may be used
during the course of design work, are also of considerable value. But
to a great extent the value of these final presentation drawings and
models depends upon using the appropriate specialists in illustration
drawing and model making. This is essential when such drawings and
models are placed before customers or used in exhibitions and

advertisements. Where scale illustrations or models are prepared there should always be an indication of scale, preferably by incorporating scale drawings or models of the human figure. On occasions illustrations may be found which, though perhaps dramatic in effect, do not really give a clear picture of the product; particularly if it is shown from an angle at which it will not be normally seen in service. Worm's-eye and bird's-eye views are, in most cases, only for worms and birds. Many engineering products, particularly large pieces of equipment are illustrated very effectively by giving three-dimensional body to normal orthographic drawings. This technique is closely related to finished architectural drawings of which plenty of examples can be found. The presentation drawing which deliberately sets out to deceive the customer, making a product seem bigger or smaller than it really is (if these qualities are relevant), is inexcusable.

7.5 WORKING WITH THE SPECIALISTS

In most modern circumstances engineering design work is undertaken by a team. The breakdown of design work between those who produce initial schemes and those who fill out these schemes, and prepare working drawings, can be regarded as one type of team activity. Unfortunately, and to the detriment of design, this technique may not always be seen in this light. The expertise involved in preparing working drawings in relation to all spectrum requirements, particularly requirements for economical manufacture, is frequently overlooked. Thus it may not be recognised that this expertise cannot be properly utilised if it is not supported by adequate information and guidance. The same requirement obtains for any other type of specialist employed in the design team. And clearly there may be other specialists besides the industrial designer.

If the industrial designer is to function satisfactorily in a design team he must have:

1. The support and goodwill of management.
2. The goodwill of his colleagues.
3. *All* the information relevant to the project: company design policy, market areas, competitor's products, available resources, preferred manufacturing methods, complete specification details, etc.

The foregoing applies whether industrial designers are employed as part of the design staff, or as consultants coming in either to tackle one particular product or to work for a company as and when required. The staff designer will be able to acquire all the knowledge he needs as he takes up his position. However, the consultant, particularly one who is called upon to undertake an urgent project, should be given the fullest information. It ought to be noted that some manufacturers are reluctant to do this. Yet they may be first to complain if the industrial designer's contribution causes an increase in production costs or does not allow efficient functioning. Sometimes matters such as design policy or even production costs are deemed to be part of management's private knowledge; not to be aired even among those in staff positions let alone those being called in to assist the staff designers. This is extremely short-sighted, both for staff and consultants. Just as a consultant must have faith in his employer, that he will be paid on completion of the work, so a management should recognise that, as an agent of the company while in its employ, a consultant will deal with the company in the strictest confidence. While any designer must be faced with tackling urgent projects at some time or another, it is important to try, even in hurried circumstances, to give an industrial designer not only all relevant details concerning the project but also enough time to appreciate company structure and attitudes. Factory and office tours are of great value here. It is also most useful if the industrial designer can become acquainted informally with those with whom he may work, particularly those who will be transmitting his ideas into working drawings. Knowledge of design office and factory procedures will also be of value.

Clearly it is vital that an industrial designer should be told how the product functions. This elementary requirement may sometimes be overlooked. Even where this is not the case, explanations may often be made on the assumption that the industrial designer is fully aware of some of the principles which may be employed. In the complexity and scope of modern engineering, the engineer who is closely concerned with and perhaps trained in one particular aspect, may not always realise that his equipment can be quite mysterious even to other engineers. Technical explanations should always begin from a simple basis.

One of the great problems faced by staff and consultant industrial designers is that, because the effectiveness of much of their work cannot be measured in physical terms as with performance aspects, it can be easily criticised. Criticism is most valuable when it is made by other designers in relation to aspects with which they are concerned. For example, if a particular form limits a performance requirement then clearly it must be challenged. Criticism is also valuable when it comes from knowledge which should have been transmitted to the designer at the beginning of the project, but which has either been overlooked or only come to hand during the course of design work. Thus a member of a marketing section might point out that a colour scheme was too close to that of a competitor. But unsupported and entirely subjective criticism of the 'I don't like it' variety is of little value. Probably the greatest offenders in this respect are members of management who may well call upon wives and secretaries usually to support purely personal opinions. But if opinions regarding appearance are needed then it is far better to approach those who fairly represent a cross-section of the envisaged markets.

On occasions, changes or additions are made to products usually due to the addition of special requirements from the customer. This is extremely likely in certain types of capital plant and equipment and can cause difficulties if a good overall appearance is to be maintained. Wherever possible the industrial designer should be advised of likely changes so that he can endeavour to uphold the standards he has helped to set. The worst type of modification is that undertaken because someone cannot resist installing at the last moment some characteristic which he believes to be especially attractive. When this occurs time and money has been wasted in employing an industrial designer. Such a modification is simply an indication of inefficient design administration.

7.6 WAYS OF USING INDUSTRIAL DESIGNERS

7.6.1. THE CONSULTANT DESIGNER

The consultant designer is probably most useful to companies which would not be able to find sufficient work to warrant a full-time employee. Working in a rather larger field than the staff designer he may bring fresher ideas to a project and be less inhibited by prevailing company attitudes. Indeed a number of engineering companies use consultants precisely for this reason. However in most cases the decision to use a consultant is based upon the fact that full time employment would be uneconomical.

When using a consultant for the first time, it is useful to choose a 'pilot project' which will help to prove his worth and introduce him to company techniques. But even on a pilot project, time should be spent in providing the consultant with the type of information outlined in the foregoing section. It is most important that good personal relationships should be established between the consultant and those with whom he will work.

It is never too soon to call in a consultant though he may not be able to begin his own work as soon as a project commences. By calling him in at the outset, he can become intimately aware of the problems involved. It must be restressed that, because design is essentially a process of synthesis, a much better product will be obtained if all requirements are recognised and worked towards at the outset. Further it is more likely that the product will be less expensive and take less time to develop. When new engineering principles are being employed, some time may be involved in proving their effectiveness for the task in mind. But while, in some cases, this preliminary work will last for a considerable period, it is useful to allow the consultant to be aware of developments. He may then be able to produce concepts of the ultimate form of the product and these can be extremely useful not only in practical terms but also in stimulating development engineers.

Preliminary design 'visuals' (pictorial concepts of the possible form of the final product), together with models help to provide such engineers with a target. Unfortunately receipt of a consultant's preliminary visuals and models is sometimes regarded as concluding his work on a project. But in fact, it should represent the beginning of a more intense collaboration between the consultant and his engineering associates; and this collaboration should last until the product has been completed.

While on occasions a consultant may be called in to assist in the design of one particular product, it is most useful to maintain the relationship subsequently. His acquired experience of company techniques can be of considerable value when other projects arise.

Further, given the opportunity, he may be able to assist improvement on other products and lead the company towards establishing a sound house style. Finally, in being allowed to maintain contact, the consultant can help to keep a company informed of industrial design developments in the world at large. In short he can be used in an advisory capacity as well as an active capacity.

7.6.2 THE STAFF-EMPLOYED INDUSTRIAL DESIGNER

The staff-employed industrial designer is likely to be found in companies having sufficient work to keep him fully occupied. While it can be argued that his experience and outlook may be more restricted by comparison with that of a consultant, the staff industrial designer is readily available when day-to-day problems arise. He can also become more familiar with company techniques. As with a consultant, he should be called in at the beginning of a project and should be allowed to maintain close contact with it throughout its duration. In order to avoid the danger of becoming inhibited by internal company pressures, the staff-employed designer should be allowed to visit exhibitions, attend conferences on industrial design and keep in touch with other industrial designers.

A broad interest in developments in all fields of design can be maintained if the staff designer is called upon to give short lectures from time to time to his engineering colleagues.

In large companies more than one industrial designer may be needed, enabling the formation of an industrial design department. Besides being available for work on current projects, an industrial design department can produce recommendations for colour and finishes, lettering, control components and so on. This activity ensures that a good aesthetic standard is maintained and that house style requirements are satisfied.

One large British organisation allows its department to arrange periodic conferences, lectures and 'design appreciation courses' for engineers. These can be extremely valuable in encouraging co-operation and extending the realisation that industrial design in engineering is not a separate activity but an integral part of the whole engineering design process.

7.7 CONCLUSION

In the commercial world it is common to encourage an improvement in industrial design terms by saying that the better-looking product will sell better. But the importance of industrial design in engineering is very much more than the importance of meeting a commercial objective. In a time span of two centuries, engineering has transformed much of our environment. It has created great benefits and the possibility of even greater benefits in the future. It has also been responsible for much ugliness, not only in our environments but also in the way in which machines have used people, as much as they have themselves been used.

A rapidly developing technology, introducing new sources of power and producing more refined devices, has in many instances helped to improve environmental and working conditions. But one need not look far to find products and equipment which could be improved by greater awareness of human values. One should not believe that an advancing technology will, by itself, create a better world either in aesthetic terms or in the broader social sense. There is a danger that, being closest to applying the results of scientific research, engineers might believe this to be the case. There could even be a greater danger in that engineers might not only overlook but actually reject humanism in the design of their products.

The saving fact is that they are themselves human. If their abilities extend to the more aesthetic aspects of design then they cannot nor should their educators allow these abilities to be atrophied. They should improve themselves by observation and practice; as much for what they gain for themselves as for what they can contribute. Those with no practical ability can also gain a great deal by taking a greater interest in the character and quality of our living and working conditions. Critical faculties will develop and a desire for improvement will follow. It will also be realised that more than commercial objectives and technological improvement is needed to make better products for people.

BIBLIOGRAPHY

Chapter One

1 DERBY, T. K., and WILLIAMS, T. I., *A Short History of Technology*, Clarendon Press (at Oxford) (1960).

Entirely technological, but essential reading especially in order to appreciate the development of materials, tools and skills available to the designer.

2 FARR, M., *Design in British Industry*, Cambridge University Press (1955).

Omits engineering design, but is a useful guide to design in the craft based industries; i.e. furniture, pottery, textiles, etc.

3 GIEDION, S., *Mechanisation takes Command*, Oxford University Press (1948).

Development of the machine and its influence upon society. Interesting illustrations of nineteenth and early twentieth century machinery; compare with architecture of the same period.

4 MUMFORD, L., *Technics and Civilisation*, Routledge & Sons Ltd. (George) (1934).

Sociological influences of technology. A book to read in a reflective mood.

5 READ, H., *Art and Industry*, Faber & Faber Ltd. (1953).

Provides a link between technical and human aspects of product design.

Chapter Two

6 CHAPANIS, A., *Research Techniques in Human Engineering*, John Hopkins Press (1959).
   To be read before setting up experiments; refined but not complex.

7 DREYFUSS, H., *The Measure of Man*, Whitney Library of Design (1959/60).
   Gives anthropometric information for U.S. groups and shows how to use it.

8 KELLERMAN, F., van WELY, P., and WILLEMS, P., *Vademecum Ergonomics in Industry*, Philips Technical Library–Cleaver-Hume Press Ltd. (1963).
   Brief but very useful guide for designers of control and display regions.

9 MCCORMICK, E. J., *Human Factors Engineering*, McGraw-Hill Book Co Inc., (1957).
   Similar to 10, but one of the first books to make a comprehensive approach to ergonomics.

10 MORGAN, C. T., COOK, J. S., CHAPANIS, A., and LUND, M. W., *Human Engineering Guide to Equipment Design*, McGraw-Hill Book Co. Inc. (1963).
   A compendium book, especially useful for the design of work regions.

Chapter Three

11 ADCOCK, C. J., *Fundamentals of Psychology*, Penguin Books Ltd. (1966).
   Readable introduction to the human mind especially in relation to perception and learning.

12 KEPES, G., *Language of Vision*, Paul Theobald, Chicago. 6th Reprint (1949).
   An artist's approach mainly to painting and graphic design but of considerable interest in substantiating much of the more scientific approaches.

13 MOHOLY-NAGY, L., *Vision in Motion*, Paul Theobald, Chicago, 5th Reprint (1956).

Another artist's approach and like the foregoing (12), stimulating reading.

14 VERNON, M. D., *Psychology of Perception*, Penguin Books Ltd. (1966).
Full study of perception based upon research.

Chapter Four

15 BIRREN, F., *Creative Colour*, Reinhold Publishing Corp., N.Y. (1961).
More for artists but illustrates different types of colour harmony.
16 GLOAG, H. L., *Colouring in Factories*, Factory Building Studies, No. 8 (Code No. 47-212-8). H.M.S.O. (1961).
Excellent brief guide to colours for machinery. Should be read in conjunction with 'The Lighting of Factories, No. 2' in the same series.
17 OPT. SOC. AMERICA (COMMITTEE ON COLORIMETRY), *The Science of Color*, Crowell Co. (Thomas, Y.), N.Y. (1953).
Refined study of colour, useful in an ergonomic context.
18 WILSON, R. F., *Colour and Light at Work*, Seven Oaks Press Ltd. (1953).
Useful introduction and general guide to colour.
19 WILSON, R. F., *Colour in Industry Today*, Allen & Unwin Ltd. (George) (1960).
Similar to the foregoing (17).

Chapter Five

20 EYSENCK, H. J., *Sense and Nonsense in Psychology*, Penguin Books Ltd. (1965).
Compare Eysenck's chapter on 'The psychology of aesthetics' with Fry's essay.
21 FRY, R., *Vision and Design*, Chatto & Windus Ltd. (1937).
Fry's 'Essay in Aesthetics' makes a useful starting point for studying a complex subject.
22 LE CORBUSIER, *The Modulor*, Faber & Faber Ltd. (1961).
Tortuous but intriguing theories presented to support a proportioning system based on the Golden Ratio and human dimension.

23 TEAGUE, W. D., *Design this Day*, Studio Publications Ltd. (1947).
Carries the reader from theory to practice.

Chapter Six

There are no books dealing with style as such. However, a wide variety of histories of architecture, furniture etc. exist and should be studied. The books (1–6) described for Chapter One are also useful.

Chapter Seven

24 ASHFORD, F. C., *Designing for Industry*, Pitman & Sons Ltd. (Sir Isaac), (1955).
Examines the aesthetics of product design and deals with practical aspects of presentation.

25 BERESFORD-EVANS, J., *Form in Engineering Design*, Clarendon Press (at Oxford) (1954).
Practical approach to handling industrial design aspects.

26 van DOREN, H., *Industrial Design*, McGraw-Hill Book Co. Inc., 2nd edition (1954).
Larger work than the foregoing but again taking a practical approach.

27 DYSON, B. H., and MAYALL, W. H., *Design and Programming for World Market*, British Productivity Council (1963).
A Collection of papers used for B.P.C. seminars and dealing with design policy, industrial design, designing for economical manufacture and design office practice.

INDEX